HE'S GONE UNDERCOVER ... YOU TIME AND MONEY—HERE ARE
THE ANSWERS TO YOUR QUESTIONS:

—How do I negotiate a deal on my car that will really
save me money?
—Are there substantial savings on last year's model?
—Are foreign cars better buys?
—Should I special-order a car?
—Is buying a demo model a good deal?
—Where will I get the best financing—dealer or bank?

And more—in this fact-filled, professional guide that turns
the biggest con into a game YOU CAN WIN!

DR. LESLIE R. SACHS is a Harvard graduate who
grew up in Chicago, where he was born in 1955.
A former college instructor with seven earned degrees
in philosophy, education, and canon law, he makes
his home in Virginia just outside of the
nation's capital.

How to Buy Your New Car for a Rock-Bottom Price

Dr. Leslie R. Sachs

A SIGNET BOOK

NEW AMERICAN LIBRARY

A DIVISION OF PENGUIN BOOKS USA INC., NEW YORK

This book is dedicated to my boyhood friends from Chicago. I hope it will help all of them to get a great deal on their next new car.

SIGNET
Published by the Penguin Group
Penguin Books USA Inc., 375 Hudson Street,
New York, New York 10014, U.S.A.
Penguin Books Ltd, 27 Wrights Lane,
London W8 5TZ, England
Penguin Books Australia Ltd, Ringwood,
Victoria, Australia
Penguin Books Canada Ltd, 10 Alcorn Avenue,
Toronto, Ontario, Canada M4V 3B2
Penguin Books (N.Z.) Ltd, 182–190 Wairau Road,
Auckland 10, New Zealand

Penguin Books Ltd, Registered Offices:
Harmondsworth, Middlesex, England

First Printing, September, 1987
14 13 12 11 10 9 8 7

 REGISTERED TRADEMARK—MARCA REGISTRADA

Printed in Canada

PUBLISHER'S NOTE
This publication is designed to provide accurate and authoritative information in regard to the subject matter covered. It is sold with the understanding that the publisher is not engaged in rendering legal, accounting or other professional service. If legal advice or other expert assistance is required, the service of a competent professional person should be sought.

Table of Contents

Acknowledgments

The author would like to express his very special thanks to Lisa M. Madigan, Susan J. Lodge, and David S. Lodge for their adventurous and warm support of this project.

The author also thanks Tamara Ehlin, Ruth Koeppel, and Denise Marcil for their publishing professionalism and their role in making this book a success.

How Dr. Sachs Helped Us Buy a Car

We decided to write this introduction to *How to Buy Your New Car for a Rock-Bottom Price* because we feel indebted to Dr. Leslie Sachs. You see, he went with us when we bought our new car and saved us over $3,000.

Like many people, we put off buying a new car, but in our case the procrastination was extreme. We were driving a 1966 Ford Falcon inherited from Amanda's Aunt Hazel, and we might still be driving it, blowing black smoke down the road, if the brakes hadn't failed on the parkway during rush hour. We hated to admit it but we *had* to look for a new car.

A few nights later we were sitting around with a couple of friends including Dr. Sachs, bemoaning our fate and hoping he'd take the hint. He did. We were a bit hesitant about beginning our search. Who wants to deal with car salesmen? Car salesmen can be slimy. We know a lot of people who have been cheated in the showroom. Do the salesmen hypnotize their customers? we wondered. But we knew Dr. Sachs was writing this book, so we felt a lot better when he offered to go car-shopping with us.

The next morning Dr. Sachs drove us out to the strip with all the dealers. We shivered in the cold beneath his open sunroof. (Everyone has their fetishes, and sunroofs are his.) We turned pale as he gunned his turbocharger. (That's his other car fetish.) Dr. Sachs explained his buying strategy. We'd go around to all the dealers and see what each had to offer in our price range. There was one car, though, that Dr. Sachs thought might fit our needs. "It's called the Sundance. It's a really cute car that's not expensive and you can get it with a turbocharger *and* a sunroof!"

"No!" Amanda said. "We could never own a car called a Sundance. It's too trendy a name."

We spent the day looking at various cars. We must have appeared fairly trustworthy because the salesmen simply noted our driver's license number and let us test drive the cars on our own. The three of us tested the Plymouth Sundance, which we drove to a Chevy dealer, parked it there, and then we all drove off to lunch in a Chevy Cavalier. After lunch we stopped by a Hyundai dealer to test drive a Hyundai Excel. We then discovered that Dr. Sachs had left his hat in one of the cars we had scattered along the strip. We began to backtrack in search of the hat, and by the time we found the hat it was clear which of the cars we wanted. (We decided to buy a Sundance.)

Then it was time to get down to dealing. Dr. Sachs advised us to let him do the talking, since we hadn't yet read his book.

Our salesman was a rotund horse trader named Vern. We've since read Dr. Sachs' book, and the tricks the salesman tried were exactly the ones described in the following pages. The salesman pulled out a sales order, marked a few figures, and showed it to us. Dr. Sachs did a quick mental calculation, crossed out the numbers, and wrote a few numbers of his own. Vern looked us straight in the eye, and with a fatherly voice told us that he was sorry—he couldn't let the car go for so little money. We looked disappointed. Dr. Sachs put on his coat. We put on our coats. The salesman spoke to his manager.

The salesman's boss came in and patiently explained to us that there was absolutely no way he could sell the car at such a low price. He jotted down a few more figures. Leslie crossed them out and slapped down a credit card.

"I see you know how to play this game!" said the manager. Vern's boss went off, and came back with the general manager, the big cheese of the operation. This guy told us our offer was below the invoice.

"Show us the invoice, then," said Dr. Sachs. To my amazement, the general manager, after a little arguing, did bring out the invoice. Dr. Sachs' last offer was $50 below it, and Leslie raised the offer by $150 and told us to sit tight.

Vern tried every trick he knew on us, but thanks to Dr. Sachs they didn't work—he will tell you all about these tricks in this book.

They finally accepted our offer and, once the deal was signed, Vern for the first time dealt with us like human beings. While we waited for various papers to be processed, we chatted about money, cars and life. They hardly even bothered us about the phony rustproofing they like to sell.

We handed the check over to the finance manager. We paid cash, but Dr. Sachs gives you advice on how to finance a new car or even buy one for no money down. The finance guy held up the sales order and laughed, saying, "Look at all the crossed out numbers on this slip. You really beat up on my salesman!"

We're very happy with our new car. We saw with our own eyes: Dr. Sachs gets a great deal on any new car. He saved us thousands, and we're sure he can save you a bundle as well. And, with *How to Buy Your New Car for a Rock-Bottom Price,* you'll also have fun while you shop for your car.

Terrance Swift and Amanda Perez

1

How They Sell You the Wrong Car and Charge Too Much for It

Congratulations! You've just bought the very best book on how to buy a new car. Clearly and simply, I'll show you how to pick the right car for your needs, and how to save as much as $4,000 on the total cost. You'll have fun, save money, and get a great car for yourself. All you need is the book in front of you!

There's nothing quite like the feeling of a new car—the shiny paint job, the fresh and supple handling, the distinctive smell of a new interior. It's a joy to drive around and show off to your neighbors and friends. You earned it, you picked it, you bought it, you enjoy it—it's part of the American dream.

But there are some rascals who would like to overcharge you for fulfilling that dream. Nineteen out of every twenty Americans pay far too much—usually thousands of dollars too much—for the cars they buy. Many of those same people bought the wrong car, a car they don't want or didn't need, because they gave in too quickly to an eager and energetic salesman. Now, however, it's your turn to play the auto-buying game and *win*. I'll tell you everything you need to know to pick the right car for yourself. I'll show you how to get that perfect deal on a car—and save you as much as $3,000 or $4,000 in the process. I'll show you every trick they'll use to overcharge you and how to laugh at the salesman's baloney. Best of all, instead of being annoyed and confused by the salespeople, you'll have lots of fun picking out your new car and hammering out a good deal. You'll find you have more control over your life as you learn how to negotiate one of the biggest purchases that you'll ever make. Just think of what you can do with the money you save!

"But the last time I bought a car, everyone was so friendly! They can't be crooks!"

Careful! Oh, sure, there are plenty of friendly car salesmen. Most of the car dealers I know are friendly. Their friendliness is one of their most useful tools in overcharging you. I've been to dozens of car dealers throughout the country, and I haven't found an honest one yet, though I've found plenty that smile nicely when they tell fibs. They're out to make money, no matter how friendly they seem, and they're willing to play tricks to do it.

"But my neighbor just bought a car, and the salesman gave him a great deal!"

Chances are your neighbor still paid too much. The same people who got overcharged usually think they got a great deal. When you get bamboozled out of $2,000 or $3,000, your natural impulse is to pretend it didn't happen. It's only human! Since most people don't really know what's going on in new car sales, they mask their uncertainty by pretending that they got a good deal. After you've read this book, you'll know the real story. You'll know exactly how to play the game, and win!

"But it's such a hassle, I just want to get it over with! Why should I bother!"

First of all, money is a reason to bother. With this book, you will most likely be able to buy a car you thought you couldn't afford. It might take you two hours to read this book, and maybe three hours to get that good deal on your car. If you save only $2,000, that's $400 an hour. Is that worth your time? I should think so!

What if you're so rich that you don't care about losing $2,000? Fine. In that case, you have your dignity to consider. Why let the salespeople snicker behind your back? You'll find that it's more fun to shop as a winner at the auto-sales game, with the deck stacked in your favor. You'll chuckle out loud when you see them use the same lies you've seen in this book, when the discount they first say is impossible is then handed to you with their gratitude that you're buying the car at all!

My Undercover Adventure: The Secret World of Car Salesmen

Selling cars is not just another job. The money involved in car sales is awesome. In large urban areas many car salesmen make $50,000 to $80,000 per year. Surprise! The salesmen might be paid on a straight commission basis, but that commission is between 15 and 35 percent of the "gross," or profit margin, on each car the dealer sells. Since the profit margin on a car may range from $400 to over $3,000, depending on how much they get you to pay, the salesman can make $1,000 or more from a single sale. If the salesman averages a commission of $500 per car and he sells two or three cars per week, he's making one heck of a lot of money. The top salesman I knew made over $12,000 a month—$144,000 a year—selling Chevrolets. He sold about 25 cars a month at a profit of $500 each, so you can see why he's a millionaire.

The sales managers—the guys who sit in small offices surrounding the salesroom floor, whispering directions to the salespeople—are often salaried in six figures. The sales managers in my area usually make about $100,000 to $125,000.

The incomes of auto salespeople are amazing, but it's a secret well kept from the general public. They don't want you to know how much money they're making off you because it would damage their ability to trick you into paying too much. It's easier for them to overcharge you if you think the salesman is just a hardworking regular guy. But, in fact, they're so well paid that you don't have to feel sorry about winning a good deal from them. After you've read this book and get your car for a good price, they'll still get their minimum commission of $100 or so, which is not bad for a few hours' work. Plus they'll still be overcharging a lot of other people who don't know what you will know. So don't feel guilty about being a winner at the bargaining game.

Another big secret about selling new cars in America is that, virtually everywhere, car salesmen operate according to a certain system designed to fool you and take your money. The system has been carefully developed to earn the auto dealers billions of dollars in extra profits per year. Many of us have a vague sense that we get overcharged at car dealers, but we shrug it away by fooling ourselves into believing, "Oh, I guess I got a pretty good deal." In the pages ahead I'll show you what a *real* good deal is, so that you'll never be unsure of yourself again. I'll show you how to play the game of keeping more money in your pocket rather than in the car dealer's stock portfolio.

The sales racket developed by the auto industry has two goals: to get you to buy a car, today, whether it's right or wrong for you; and to get you to pay several thousand dollars more than you need to pay. Dealers have so many different ways of fooling you that it is not enough to catch one or two of their tricks. You need a full, clear picture of what's going on, of all the things a car dealer will say and do. Once you finish this book, it will be easy and even fun to get a great deal. You'll giggle to yourself as they try one phony lie after another. And the dealer will respect and admire you for going home with a great car at a great price.

How did I learn so much about the auto-sales racket? I went to the source and learned the game from its master players. I went undercover as a car salesman at new car dealers in the Washington, D.C., area where I live. At the first dealer I took a special week-long training course for salesmen where the whole sales game was explained to me in great detail. I practiced my techniques on the showroom floor and tried to discover whether or not there was any way to sell cars honestly (I found that the managers won't let you). Since my experience of going undercover, I've visited dozens of car dealers, both in the Washington area and around the country, shopping with friends for new cars. Just about everywhere I find the same games and the same attempts to overcharge the customer. The major exception I found is car dealers in rural areas, where the staff tries to keep a good relationship with the neighbors. In the country, salespeople are nervous about playing games that might backfire on them. But even friendly country car dealers will still play a few games to make a profit. In the metropolitan area the dealer often plays the sales game to the hilt, since he counts on never seeing you again.

It's easy to get hired as a car salesman. They're always looking for new people. (Check the want ads in any big city newspaper.) If you're a lively talker, just walk in the door wearing a good suit, tell them you're greedy and that you have a little sales experience, and they'll probably hire you. After all, you're usually not on salary, so it's no big deal to give a chance to someone new. Of course I didn't tell them I have a doctorate, or that I was going to write a book on car sales. They told me, "Leslie, you're going to be great! You talk so easily, and you've got such a sincere face. You'll make a mint!" Some of my friends still tell me I was stupid to quit. After all, I passed up a gold mine!

In many ways, auto sales is the American dream come true. You can make a fortune with no education, no special skills, just your own personality and gift of gab. You walk in the door, get hired on the spot, and almost immediately you're earning over $1,000 a week. Too bad it's so crooked.

If car salesmen make so much money, why is it so easy to get a job selling cars? First of all, although lots of people have had jobs in "sales," it's hard to find first-class swindlers. People are naturally cautious when making a major purchase, and as a car salesman you have only a small amount of time to convince the customer to trust you with a significant portion of his or her life's earnings. That takes skill.

Secondly, it is very stressful to deceive people all day. If car sales involved simply convincing someone to buy the product, it could be a respectable and enjoyable job. Car sales is stressful because the salesman must lie to each one of his customers. He must look at the public as an adversary, and his own income (and his manager's approval) depends on his ability to bamboozle the human being in front of him. Even people who are greedy as a rule may find it hard to sell cars because of the stress. Some car salesmen burn out after a few months and slip into drink or drugs. Still others take the money they've made and go into another business after a year or two. So there's always room for someone new.

Whenever I quit a dealer, I found that it took guts to leave a $60,000 a year job, no matter how unappealing the dishonesty. I would dream about money for weeks afterward.

While undercover as a car salesman, I sometimes played the game to the hilt just to gauge the success of the auto-sales game. At other times, I used guerrilla tactics to blow the dealer's con game right out of the water.

I remember a time I dealt with a young family—a military guy, his wife, and their two-year-old little girl. Their dream car was a red hatchback Chevy Cavalier. After reviewing their budget, I realized they could only afford it at a deep discount price, without the $3,500 extra the dealer wanted to charge. The couple was quite sweet and willing to go along with anything I said.

After talking over the situation with the manager, I was ordered to sell the family the *wrong* car—a Chevette— at $2,000 more than necessary, rather than sell them the car they wanted at a good price. Given that the couple only had a limited amount of money, the management's objective was to sell them the cheapest possible car at the highest possible price. Looking at that cute little girl as she cuddled in her daddy's arms, I saw a picture of families all across America getting cheated by car dealers. So I took the man aside, explained the whole crooked game to him, and sent him on his way to buy his dream car at another dealer.

Pressure to Buy *Today*:
Why it's Hard to Shop for a Car

You might be tempted to pop around to a car dealer or two before you read any further, just to "have a look" at some new cars and find out something about prices. Beware, this is a risky business! Most customers who walk into a showroom think they are just looking, and many of those same people drive home in a new car. Car salesmen are experts at turning the prospective customer into a new car owner. Most of the customers who get hooked in this way think it was their own decision: "I went to the car dealer just looking, and you won't believe it, it's the craziest thing, but I bought a car! It's parked out front right now!"

Salesmen have prepackaged sales pitches they use to convince you to buy a car. One of the best is that somehow today is a special day—my, how lucky you are!—the manager is out of his mind giving discounts, and we have a *very* special deal for you that is *only* good if you buy the car today. This is hokum. Any deal that is possible today will be available tomorrow as well.

You can understand why the salesmen are so interested in selling you a car *today*. Unless you buy a car, they don't make any money. Managers inspire their salesmen with statistics like the following:

A. If you don't sell the customer today, he's lost.

B. Three out of every four people who walk in the door will buy a new car within the next 72 hours.

C. Most customers don't see more than four car salesmen before buying a new car.

Many car salesmen see nobody or only one customer a day during the week, and maybe two or three on a Saturday. That's why they appear so eager when they approach you. You're either a zero to them or a possible thousand dollars in their pocket. A great car salesman will sell a car to one out of every three customers he sees. So when he sees you walk through the door, the salesman thinks, "Here's a one-out-of-three chance at $500 or even $1,000 in my pocket. Let's go for it!"

When you walk into a new car showroom, you're an important person. Your arrival is noted in a daily record, and the salesman who talks to you will have to give a full report to the manager on what you said and why you wouldn't buy a car. They may be friendly, they may be subtle, but there is usually some pressure underneath their slick approach. (If there is no pressure on you, the salesman is new, the manager is disorganized, or both of them are momentarily weary of playing the sales game.) But *you* are really master of the auto showroom. You can get the great deal that they don't want you to have, and you can drive the salesmen completely crazy!

Few people walk into car dealers unless they are seriously interested in buying a car in the immediate future. As a customer, you may think you are just looking and not quite yet ready to buy a car, but every car salesman is trained to disbelieve you. If a customer comes in and says he is just looking, the salesman thinks: "Here's a customer who wants to buy a car but doesn't know what he wants and is a little nervous about the whole thing. But he's got the money, otherwise he wouldn't have come here in the first place. I need to seduce this person, relax him, put him in a car and send him home. He doesn't know what he's doing, so it'll be easy to give him some tiny discount and convince him he was lucky to get some special deal *today*!"

The salesman always sees you as a means of practicing to become a better salesman. He treats you as if he's got one shot to sell you, with a possible $1,000 for him if he wins. If he doesn't sell you a car, he and the manager discuss what they might have said to make you spend more time in the showroom. They know that you will probably buy a car from one of the next two or three salesmen you meet, someone who will succeed where they failed.

You probably consider yourself a rational person, someone who is hard to manipulate. You don't think of yourself as someone who can be bulldozed by a sleazy salesman. But it happens to the best of us—I've seen it over and over again. When you're in a car dealership, those swindlers can make it seem so good, so real, so enticing, that you can wind up buying a car in spite of yourself. *"Hey, I just went to this car dealer for a look, and I met this really nice salesman, and, well, I just decided to take a new car home!"*

One of the ways to pick up on a car dealer's routine is to go to a dealership when you're *not* interested in buying a car. You'll find it to be a pain in the neck, with the salesman asking you all sorts of questions and badgering you until he's convinced you're not a buying customer. There are very few people who hang around car dealers just for fun, just to window-shop; the sales game is too much of a hassle if you're not playing it yourself.

Understanding Auto Salespeople

The funny thing is, I've enjoyed, if not respected, the men and women I've met while working at dealerships. I will be talking a lot about what a bunch of swindlers and crooks they all are, but that is just to put you in the right mood for playing "auto poker" with these highly trained chiselers. I am telling the truth about their tricks and lies, and you will see that for yourself when you next go shopping for a car. While undercover, I developed some affection for the crazy world of auto-sales hustlers. Today, after having become an experienced and aggressive auto shopper, somehow I still like these crooked clowns.

For one thing, auto salespeople are really individualists— mavericks, renegades, terribly funny guys who don't like bureaucracy. They're really nice people except that they're trying to overcharge you by $3,000 so they can put an extra grand in their own pockets. Their greed is real, but so is their sense of humor.

Some of them like cars, or sales, or they don't know any other way to make $80,000 annually. You really can't blame them. How many people go to law school for just the same reason? Moreover, there's something refreshing about their kind of greed. Unlike respectable people who make $80,000 per year hatching financial schemes on the 13th floor of some plush office building, auto salespeople are out there wheeling and dealing on the asphalt lot with just their mismatched neckties and their own gift of gab to help them.

A car salesman is playing a poker game at which he often hits the jackpot. Because you've read this book, you get to keep the jackpot for yourself *and* get a new car in the bargain. The salesman won't take it personally (you win some, you lose some); in fact, he'll respect you for being a good player. So have fun, and if you need to, remind the salesman, "Look, it's only money!"

2

Picking the Right Car for You

Maybe you know exactly what car you want. In that case, be sure the dealer doesn't try and convince you to buy something else, because that's what he has in stock or that's what gives him a better profit margin. If you're like most people, it can take some time to pick and choose the right car to buy.

Even if you don't have much money, and you would be content with basic, reliable transportation, it's still worth a little fuss to get a car that you're happy with. If you're like most people, the car that you buy will become a big part of your life. You'll spend a lot of time in it. People will get to identify you by your car. Even if you know you can't afford your dream Maserati, it's worth your while to spend the time to find the best possible car in your price range and to get the right options, the ones that will make *you* happy.

Your car is part of your self-image and the image you project to others—it makes a statement to people. If you get a car you like, you'll also find that it's less of a burden when you have to go on a long drive or play chauffeur for your next-door neighbor's kids. Remember, too, that with all the financial tricks I'm showing you, you can get a much nicer car than you thought you would originally. It's well worth the effort to pick carefully!

I'm not going to recommend specific cars to you. I'm a firm believer that when you buy a car, you should buy what you really want and not worry about what other people think or recommend. When you're spending this much money, it's not a time to please other people; it's a time to please yourself and the members of your family who will be using the car with you. So what if something "just as good" is $3,000 cheaper! If you've got the money and are comfortable spending it, fulfill your dreams.

The way I'd like to help you pick a car is by helping you obtain accurate information. You may have some preconceived notions about cars, or ideas based on past experience that no longer apply. It's worth a look at the basic issues that go into the choice of a new car. You can decide which ones are important, or you can completely forget about them all and just decide based on how *cute* the car is. But at least if you're going to buy a car for its cuteness, you'll understand better why you made your choice.

While you're thinking about buying a new car, you can start looking at cars on the street. If something catches your eye, try to notice the model name so that you can make a closer examination at a dealership.

Why Buy a New Car?

Buying a new car is not the greatest investment. After all, the minute you drive it away from the dealer it decreases in value a thousand dollars or more. In strictly business terms, it's better to buy a good, late-model used car from some person who got sick of his new car after four months and decided to get rid of it.

But with a brand-new car, part of what you get (or hope you get) is the added reliability of a car that came fresh from the factory. If you buy a used car, even a car that is only one year old, you always have reason to be suspicious. *"Why did the last guy who owned it get rid of it? Is it a lemon?"* New cars always come with a warranty, which lets you sleep a bit more easily.

Part of owning a new car is just the thrill, the fun, and the prestige. Who hasn't wanted to own a new car? So, eventually, most Americans break down and get one. It's fun, it's exciting: I agree. But you don't want to lose a lot of money to the snakes that slither through the showrooms and dealerships of America.

So, you buy a new car for its reliability and for the fun of it. If you keep it awhile, it becomes a reasonable investment, especially if you maintain it properly, keep your service records, and then resell it as the thoughtful "original owner."

How Much New Car Can You Afford?

This is not an easy question, for two reasons:

1. Until you understand the auto-sales game, you don't really know how much a new car costs. Since I'm saving you $3,000 or $4,000 on your overall expense for a new car, this changes the kind of car you can afford. The salesman is of no help here. Asking a salesman how much you can afford to pay for a car is like asking a pickpocket how much he hopes to take from your wallet.

2. Even if you think you know how much you want to spend on a car, you're probably wrong. When you fall in love with a car, the money doesn't matter, and you'll find that your ideas will change. I had a friend who insisted she wanted only "an $8,000 car." I showed her a number of $8,000 cars. What did she buy? A $13,000 convertible. If you say you want a monthly payment of $250, the typical salesman will think you can afford at least $325 per month, and he'll probably be right. You will pay a lot more than you think when you see a car that you really like.

How much car can you buy? Think of how much cash you want to put down and the value of the old car, if you have one, that you want to apply toward a new one. Then, as a rough rule of thumb, consider that you'll have to pay about $25 per month, varying slightly with the interest rate, for every $1,000 of car that you want to finance. So, if you've got $1,000 in cash, a $1,500 rustwagon that you want to trade, and you can afford payments of $250 per month, that means you can make the equivalent of $2,500 in a down payment, and finance

$10,000 ($250 [your monthly payment] divided by $25 [monthly cost of borrowing $1,000] equals 10, allowing you to borrow 10 times $1,000 or $10,000). Congratulations, you can buy a $12,500 car!

Given the nature of the auto-sales game, it's still not easy to know *which* car you can afford, since the dealer plans on charging you $3,000 or so more, for the car and all the "extras," than you really need to pay. After reading this book, you will in fact pay from $400 to $2000 less than the factory sticker price on most American cars (or a bit more for imports) and save a bundle on the "extras" that you will avoid.

Your New Car: Issues to Consider

Your public library is an excellent source for a preliminary look at cars. The reference librarian will be able to point out to you the consumer magazines that discuss, rate, and review various points on particular cars, such as *Car and Driver* and *Motor Trend,* which regularly review new cars, and the dry but helpful *Consumer Reports.* Another good source is AAA, the American Automobile Association. If you are an AAA member, at AAA offices you can look over the AAA reviews of quite a few of the available models.

When you are considering various car models, note the large number of "corporate twins": cars that are essentially identical but sold under different nameplates in different branches of the same car company. The Mercury Capri is essentially the same as the Ford Mustang; the Plymouth Sundance is the Dodge Shadow; and the Cadillac Cimarron is not only the Oldsmobile Firenza but also the Buick Skyhawk, the Pontiac Sunbird, and the Chevrolet Cavalier (though the Cadillac is $6,000 more than the Chevrolet).

If you are shopping for a car at the beginning of the model year—looking for a 1988 car in the fall of 1987—you will find that many of the new cars haven't yet been reviewed. In many cases, however, the model has not changed greatly from the previous year, so you can use the previous year's reviews as a guide.

Ultimately, it will be a question of your own judgment: when you see a car you think you might like, touch it, feel it, and drive it. After doing this with four or five cars, you will know the one that is right for you.

American or Foreign?

There is a common perception that American cars are of lower quality than imports. I believe this is no longer the case. This is important because, in some cases, American cars are a better bargain than their foreign counterparts.

It is true that American cars went through some terrible years, especially 1977–82. Detroit produced a lot of garbage cars; smugness and lack of quality control nearly ruined the American auto industry. But people in Detroit fought hard to turn that around, and in large measure they succeeded. I am quite amazed at the quality of some recent American cars, especially considering the price. The rigors of competition from high-quality foreign cars gave Detroit the kick in the pants it needed to produce good cars, and American automakers are now at least meeting the foreign challenge.

The reputation of a car is often a couple of years behind the actual reality. Many car buyers remember reading in the early 1980s about the advanced quality of Japanese and some European cars over American cars, and that opinion has become fixed in their minds. This image of foreign car quality has allowed dealers in foreign cars to practice outrageous price gouging, that is, arbitrarily adding $1,000, $2,000, $3,000, or more to the price of cars and selling them to the public with this bonus of pure profit. Such price gouging was encouraged by the early 1980s quotas limiting Japanese imports, thus making the restricted number of Japanese cars more expensive for their buyers.

Foreign-car dealers have capitalized on their superior image for so long that they are simply overpriced. Many foreign cars are still quality products, of course, and some are still good value for the money. There are many good reasons for choosing a foreign car, but don't be captive to the outdated perception that only foreign cars are reliable. Today, it's just as classy and sophisticated to own a fine American car as it is to own a foreign one. The quality is there in American machinery to match the foreign competition.

With many foreign cars, there's the thrill of the exotic and unusual, ranging from a modestly priced Toyota SR5 to a pricey Lamborghini. Some foreign cars are so fine and beautiful, they make your heart race. By all means, if a foreign car is right for you, buy it. On the other hand, you may prefer to take advantage of the wider range of options available on American cars, and also to benefit from the patriotic feeling of buying a homegrown automobile. The choice between American and foreign is one area of car-buying where you should trust your feelings completely.

There is one drawback to buying some imports that you should consider, especially if you are on a tight budget. With many imported cars, you will have a hard time getting parts and service. Many foreign-car owners have had the sad experience of breaking down in a strange place only to find that the nearest qualified service center was 50 or more miles away. You might experience delay or the impossibility of being serviced without an expensive long-distance tow.

Repairs can cost more on foreign cars, too. You don't always have wide availability of parts, and parts can be more expensive. Sometimes you have to use specialized mechanics who are the only ones with expertise in your type of car. Regular auto-repair centers may not have the proper tools. This may result from the foreign company's reluctance to sell the tools to any but its own authorized mechanics, who therefore can charge a premium for their services.

With the more popular foreign cars such as Volkswagens,

Nissans, and Toyotas, the availability of parts and service is getting better, although the prices for repair parts are still higher than for American cars. But the final word is what pleases you: if you really have your heart set on a European Grand Turtle and are willing to spend the extra money and time it might require to get it adequately serviced, you should certainly buy it. A car is for fun—do anything you want so long as you can reasonably afford it and understand what you are getting into.

Manual or Automatic?

Much of the decision between manual and automatic is simply personal. Some people love to fuss with gears—we feel it makes driving more interesting, and we feel closer to the car and to the road when we drive a stick shift. Others find a stick shift an annoyance, an unnecessary hassle that they would prefer to avoid.

A stick shift, especially one with a tachometer (the gauge that measures engine speed), allows you to drive more precisely, to gear your engine to just the right level, and to save on gas mileage. Automatic transmissions used to eat a lot of gas; however, there are currently more efficient ones that don't use much more gas than the manual.

The other major factor to consider is whether there will be someone else driving the car. In case you're ever sick, sleepy, injured, or drunk, another person can always take over if you own a car with an automatic transmission. With manual transmission, however, you will have to be sure that family members and other likely drivers know how to use the stick and clutch.

Front Wheel Drive

With the early 1980s front-wheel-drive technology came into its golden age, and the older rear-wheel-drive cars are largely being phased out. Front-wheel drive

(FWD) is what the name denotes: the power flowing through the front wheels rather than through the drive train to the back wheels, as in the old days. Now that automakers know how to make FWD cars well, there are a number of advantages to FWD that benefit today's drivers. A car with FWD uses power more efficiently; it holds the road better in ice, snow, and rain, making the car much safer; and FWD is less wearing on certain parts of the car. You will be able to plow through a snowstorm in a car with the superior traction of FWD, whereas older American cars will be sitting in a ditch.

There are certain advantages to the older type of rear-wheel-drive car. FWD has the drawback of lessening the effect of torque, or twisting power, generated by the drive train. Torque is a bit hard to explain, but basically it's the combined feeling of how your car both moves forward and grabs the road at the same time. On dry pavement, and for some performance cars, the torque of a rear-wheel-drive car can be preferable. Big eight-cylinder engines produce the kind of torque that make rear-wheel drive almost a necessity. Most European luxury cars, moreover, such as the Mercedes and the Volvo, are maintaining the rear-wheel-drive tradition and doing so with great quality. The Saab is a notable exception, being Europe's foremost FWD automobile.

If you like the feel of a traditional eight-cylinder American car, such as the Plymouth Gran Fury, or if you're getting a performance car such as BMW or Camaro, feel free to get rear-wheel drive. But do recognize that FWD is the wave of the future. This is important to consider for the simple reason that cars with FWD will hold their value much better. Detroit is not putting much energy into developing its remaining rear-wheel-drive cars, and some of them will be phased out over the next few years.

With any new car, ask the salesperson if it is front- or rear-wheel drive. Some vehicles, especially rough-duty trucks and some impressive Subarus, can be driven with power flowing through all four wheels for extra traction.

The Passenger/Cargo Question

Do you want to seat two people, four people, or more? Hatchback, wagon, or truck?

Two-seater cars are gaining in popularity, and I'll agree that some of them, like the Pontiac Fiero, are terribly fun and cute. But before you get one, you should seriously consider if you can afford to *not* have space to fit a third friend in the car. If your two-seater is a second car for you, you should be all set. But be sure to think about whether or not having only two seats might be inconvenient at times.

When you do have a backseat, it is worth taking a minute to notice how much room there is for the rear passengers. The rear leg room can be positively miniscule when the front seats are all the way back, especially in sports cars. You may not have adult passengers in the backseat very often, or you may like sports cars so much that you don't care how cramped the people in the back feel. Just so long as you know what you're getting yourself into before you buy the car!

In choosing a two-door versus a four-door, the major consideration is how often you'll have people climbing into the backseat. Even if there is a lot of leg room for back passengers once they are inside, it is simply more comfortable for people—especially for those who are elderly or less agile—to enter the backseat through a rear door than by dipping in behind the front seat. On the other hand, even in a large car, the two-door style lends a sportier, less conservative image.

The amount of cargo you haul is an issue in buying a car, too. If you decide to spend all your money on a new car, you might have to move when you can't pay the rent, so it will be important to have a car that can carry your belongings upon eviction. Some features can turn even a very small car into a quite handy item of transport. If you're torn between convenience and performance, there might be some middle way to make you happy. In my previous sports car, for example, the combination of a rear hatchback and a backseat that folded forward gave me quite a lot of carrying room—which meant that my friends always called me when they needed to move something. That, of course, is the risk of owning a cargo-carrying vehicle.

The station wagon is truly one of the great all-American vehicles. But it's worthwhile to note that today's station wagons come in all sizes, including small and mid-sized versions for smaller families and more moderate cargo needs. The Ford Taurus wagon, moreover, has given this class of vehicle some Space Age styling. Also on a par with station wagons in usefulness are the new minivans, begun by Dodge and Plymouth. If you are considering a big station wagon but won't usually be traveling with a lot of people or cargo, remember that large, empty wagons don't hold the road as well as smaller ones.

One of the things I've noticed is that many people don't buy a minivan or truck because they need them; they buy them because they like them and the image of driving them. I think that's fine—it's fun to pull up to an elegant hotel in a spiffy new jeep.

Think about your next vehicle and how it would fit in with your life-style. I know those little pickup trucks are cute, but do you really want one as your only car? There's one city dweller I know who always owns a pickup truck in addition to his other cars. He explained to me that because he grew up on a farm, life is just not complete without a pickup truck.

It's worthwhile to consider if some alternative car to the one you think you want might meet your needs. There's no substitute for just taking a good look at the cars available to see if there isn't a car that's just right for you.

Should You Special-Order a Car?

It used to be that most people would special-order cars. The showroom would only have a few models. Once you had decided to buy one, the dealer would slowly go over the brochure with you, and you would order a car from the factory with the exact color combinations and options that you wanted. A few weeks later, your car would arrive.

Some people don't like to buy a car off the lot. After all, some other customer might have taken it for a test drive—you don't know who has been sitting in it. Seriously, such hesitations are not reasonable. Whether you special-order a car or not, several people will have sat in the car and driven it brief distances, to get it on and off the truck or to confirm that it is in running condition.

What about getting the exact car you want? *"This is the car I want, the color and everything is fine, except that it doesn't have the two-tone ashtrays I was hoping for."* It is true that one dealer might not have the right car, but if you live near a major metropolitan area with a lot of car dealers, *somewhere* in town is the car you want. It's just a matter of looking. In the rare case where the car you want can't be found locally, you might consider special-ordering it, but you should know that there are drawbacks. For one thing, it takes a long time. The dealer will promise two or three weeks, but the managers always tell the salespeople to lie about this. The wait could actually be eight weeks or more. The salesman just has to take a phone call from you every week or so and promise, "It's on the way." Once the dealer has your deposit, he has you on a leash, and the actual delivery of the car is a low priority. The dealer just has to wait until it shows up.

The major problem with special-ordering a car is that you don't get to test drive it before you buy it. Each car is really put together in its individual way. There are all sorts of little quirky things about the way a car handles, and you should really *like* the way a particular car feels before you buy it.

The dealer will lie to you, too, and tell you that the price on a special-order car can't be negotiated as easily, but this isn't true. A special-order car can even be slightly cheaper because the dealer doesn't have to pay "rent" to keep it on his lot until he sells it.

I feel that there is something of raw pleasure in finding a car on the lot, beating on the salesman's head to get the price down, and taking the car home. It's just not as much fun negotiating for a car you haven't seen.

Special Savings on Demonstrators?

A demonstrator car, or "demo," is a car that has been used by a member of the dealership staff. One of the benefits of working at a car dealer is always having a new car to drive around in. The salesmen, managers, finance people, and a few others can take one of the new cars home and use it whenever they're not at the dealer. The cars aren't supposed to be taken on long trips, but otherwise the salesman can use it as his own. It is parked on the dealer's lot, and remains for sale, anytime the salesman is present. So if you want a car with a peach interior, and it turns out to be a demo of another salesman, someone will page him and tell him to roll that car up pronto.

The demos are picked out of the regular stock inventory. Some of them get a lot of mileage while the salesman is using them—2,000 or 3,000 or more. The salesmen are supposed to pamper their demos, but most salesmen don't really care and drive their demos like maniacs.

Many people think that it is a good deal to buy a demo because it is an almost-new car that can be bought at a huge discount. This is completely wrong, because you can almost always buy a brand-new car for less than what the average customer pays for a demo. Dealers do give discounts on demos, but they tend to give piddling ones of a few hundred dollars, discounts that are less than the discount you can negotiate on a brand-new model. Although in theory they should let the demo go for much less money, they will keep it for a customer they can fool into buying it as a demo with a "big" discount that is actually only a little discount.

You should only buy a demo if it has the exact combination of colors and options that you want. You will have to press just as hard for a good discount, however.

Last Year's Model: Is There a Savings?

Yes, but not as much as you might think. Once again, as is the case with demos, the dealer can get some customers to buy last year's model with the idea that a small discount is a great opportunity. The dealer will get a refund of at least 5 percent of the price from the manufacturer whenever he sells one of last year's models. The dealer's costs for last year's model are reduced by 5 percent ($500 off a $10,000 car). You can therefore negotiate an additional $500 off the price, but this price is still much less than the car's decrease in value.

What Time of Year Is Best to Buy a Car?

The model year for autos begins in September. Certain cars, of course, may be introduced earlier or later than the official new car kickoff in September, depending on Detroit's production schedule. But, in general, the new 1989s appear in September 1988. Even after the new cars appear, a few cars from the previous model year will still be at the dealer lot until Christmas or even later.

Almost anytime is a good time to buy a car. The dealer pays the manufacturer almost the same amount for the car throughout the model year, excepting the case of announced price increases at the factory, so the sharp customer can get the same good deal on a car anytime, anywhere. The best time to buy a car is when *you're* ready. In the strictly financial sense, you're best off buying a car at the beginning of the model year, when you will own it for a whole year before it begins to depreciate, but there is no sense in rushing into things before you're ready.

There is really no such thing as a "sale" at a car dealer. Really. I'll explain later how some of the sale gimmicks work. But the important thing to remember is that all the sale advertisements are making offers to you that are worth less than the amount you can win by just going in and pounding on them to give you a good deal. When you get to the bottom line, you will be far beyond any sale that the dealership can offer.

There is one kind of sale that *can* make a difference, however, and that is one in which the manufacturer has, in some way, cut its cost to the dealer, meaning that you can negotiate the price down even further. Most of these price cuts are secret: the factory wants to push a certain car, and so gives the dealers an incentive to sell them. You can assume there is a secret reduction if a car is very unpopular and the dealer's lot is full of them. If you learn that the *manufacturer* is cutting prices to the dealer, you can use this information as a basis for your own bargaining.

Manufacturers have given extra discounts in recent years mainly by lowered financing, which has a net effect of putting a few hundred extra dollars in your pocket. Almost all dealers will give you "5.5 percent financing," or whatever financing rate you want, because they can take part of the profit margin on the car and use that money to lower the financing to a rate that makes you happy. This is just a shuffle and the customer doesn't really save any money. It's a classic sucker routine that works: many people will happily pay the dealer an extra $3,000 for the car just so they can say, "Wow! I got 5.5 percent financing!" The 5.5 percent is real, in a sense, but the few hundred dollars the sucker saved in interest is nothing compared to the extra thousands he paid for the car.

In recent auto-sales history, there have been some real opportunities for the consumer when the low interest rate is paid for by the *manufacturer*. The discount is genuine when it is publicly advertised as "factory financing." Yet many customers still don't save money because, in their happiness at getting good financing, they pay way too much for the car.

With factory financing at a low rate, you should be able to get the full discount I will describe, *and* benefit from the low-factory financing, though it will take some pounding on the crooked salesmen. They'll say to themselves, and probably to you as well, "Come on, you're getting such a low interest rate, you can afford to pay a little extra for the car!"

In the usual sense, there is never really a "sale" at any car dealer. You should buy a car when you are ready to, and be confident that you can get a good deal anytime, anywhere.

3

Seven Decisive Features of a New Car

As you look over this list of features on new cars, there's a question of what *you* want as well as what to look for objectively in a car. Some of these factors will be important to you, and others may not be significant at all. When the people in Detroit decide how to orient a car to a segment of the market, the following are the elements they think about.

Safety

Automobile safety has not exactly been a priority for the auto industry. One of the reasons for this is that the auto-buying public does not seem to consider safety an important issue.

The safety issue really went out the window at the time of the mid-1970s gasoline shortages. At that time, the public developed a great appetite for small cars, notably Japanese ones, with very good gas mileage. The major factor in better gas mileage has been the use of light-weight materials in auto construction. A lighter car obviously requires less energy to move. The other side of a lighter car, though, is that it is significantly less safe in an accident.

There are two major factors in auto safety. One is the sheer bulk and weight of the materials of which the car is made. A large, classic American car, such as the Lincoln

Town Car or Buick Regal, is safer than the typical light-weight subcompact, such as the Toyota Tercel or Chevrolet Sprint. Year after year, statistics have shown that your chances of surviving an accident are much better if you are in a larger and heavier car.

The other major factor in auto safety is the structural design of the car. One car may have more structural integrity than another of equal weight and breadth so that, in an accident, the metal crumples in ways that are less likely to harm the occupants. Some car engines are mounted so that they drop downward during head-on impact, thus absorbing much of the shock that would otherwise strike those in the front seat.

Some bumpers can absorb more shock than others. Many modern cars have weak, "two-and-one-half-mile" bumpers that can only withstand a collision at that speed before suffering damage. Some cars have stronger, "five-mile" bumpers that can withstand much more forceful collisions. The speeds sound absurdly low, but a collision at 30 or 40 miles per hour will result in significantly less damage to the five-mile-bumper car, and thus to its occupants.

For many car buyers, safety is not at all important. "If your number is up, there is nothing you can do." But if safety is important to you, you should consider avoiding the smaller cars. You should consider whether your increased safety in a larger car might be worth a few extra dollars each month spent on gas.

Some of the options available to you can increase your car's safety. Anyone who's driven through bad weather will tell you the virtues of having a rear-window defogger, which is now mandatory in some states, especially in the cold and wintry North. Your state's Department of Motor Vehicles will tell you what equipment is required on new cars registered in your state. Dealers in your area will have their cars equipped according to minimum local standards, but be careful, if you are shopping out of state, to get a car that meets *your* state's requirements.

Many accidents involve rear-end collisions, and it has been shown that bigger brake and taillights, and the new midpoint brake lights mounted above the regular taillights (required since 1986), reduce the likelihood of rear-end accidents.

Good tires also improve safety. One of your options on a new car may be premium, top-of-the-line tires; take them if you can. When the time comes to get new tires, get the best tires you can afford. They may save your life and give you a more comfortable ride.

You should feel free to ask the salesman for information on the safety of a car model you are considering. He can point out what features of the car were designed with safety in mind and, if the car is one of the safer ones, may be able to show you a magazine article that discusses the safety of the particular model itself. *Consumer Reports*, available in your library, carries regular features on automobile-safety tests. Members of the American Automobile Association (AAA) can also benefit from AAA reports on various car models at the local AAA office. Given the expense and infrequency of crash and other safety tests, written safety evaluations are usually about earlier models of the car you are considering. So be aware that engineering changes in new cars may have altered the relevance of the evaluations that you read.

"I would get a convertible if I wasn't so worried about it rolling over." Don't worry. Convertibles have a much lower center of gravity, which means that it's much harder for them to roll over. If you want a convertible, go ahead and buy it. If you want safety, just buy a big one.

Reliability

Overall, new cars are getting more and more reliable as the manufacturers have realized that what the buyer hates most of all is hassle. People are willing to pay thousands more for a car that won't bother them by breaking down. In the last couple of years, some Japanese and European cars have maintained an impressive record of reliability, notably Hondas and BMWs, although many American cars are now rivaling them in overall quality. There's an overall image, as I've said, that "imported car" means "quality," but this is simply hype. For overall comfort and value, the American cars of the late 1980s, such as the Pontiac 6000, the Mercury Topaz, and the Chrysler New Yorker, are worthy rivals of foreign competitors.

In looking at the reliability of new cars, you're at a bit of a disadvantage in looking at the current model year. If you're thinking about buying a three-year-old used car, it is easy to find out how other cars of that model and year have fared. With a new car, you might get some impression by looking at the repair frequency required for similar models in previous years, but every year is fundamentally different. The manufacturer may have increased the quality control on the assembly line or added some new feature that is gumming up the whole works. Once again, when you want information on reliability statistics, your reference librarian can direct you to *Consumer Reports* and other appropriate publications.

Most new cars are fairly decent for the first 30,000 miles, when cars tend to experience their first need for large-scale repairs. So at least for a couple of years, you should be riding around in style and trouble-free.

If you're shopping for a car, it's good to ask the salesman about reliability. If the car is known for its reliability, he may have an article or two handy to prove it to you. If it's not a reliable car, he may have nothing more than words. Though if he doesn't have written evidence, it's not necessarily bad: a lot of salesmen are just ill-prepared.

Economy

There are two types of economy to consider when buying a car. One has to do with the actual price of the car, and the second has to do with the cost of running and maintaining it.

With regard to the price of the car, some new imports such as the Yugoslavian Yugo and the Korean Hyundai have captured the bottom range in the current market.

American cars have some good values in the under $9,000 price range, especially from Plymouth and Dodge. Very good value and selection are available in the under $14,000 price range, though the American car consumer has the option of a $25,000 Cadillac as well. You can usually achieve a greater discount in bargaining for an American car than a foreign one.

Japanese imports, theoretically ranging from under $8,000 to the $20,000 sports cars from Nissan and Toyota, will often be more expensive than advertising suggests. Japanese car makers tend to ship high percentages of their inventory fully equipped with expensive options, so you will be hard-pressed to find the stripped-down model with the "come-on" price. You will also find many dealers asking for—and getting—thousands more than the factory sticker, especially on Hondas.

European imports include some nice Renaults and Volkswagens under $10,000, and a good selection in the $10,000 to $25,000 range, including Peugeot, Saab, Volvo, and the entry-level Porsche. Europeans also offer exotic cars for people with money to burn, from a $40,000 Jaguar to a $160,000 Rolls Royce.

With regard to gas-mileage economy, smaller and lighter foreign cars have the edge. A few small American cars, such as the Chevrolet Sprint and Nova (the result of collaboration between America's General Motors and Japan's Toyota), are also good gas-economy cars. The bigger cars, however, have an improving mileage profile, even mid-sized family cars, such as the Ford Taurus and Dodge Lancer, thanks to new technology. With the lower oil prices of the mid-1980s, Americans seemed to lose their concern about the price of gas. Really big cars that use a lot of gas, classic eight-cylinder Lincolns and Buicks, are selling very well.

The other major economy factor is repair costs, and here, once again, American cars have an edge, with the wider availability of inexpensive parts and labor. Parts and labor costs for the more popular Japanese cars, the Nissans and Toyotas, have greatly moderated, but the price-per-repair edge is still with the homegrown machinery.

Usefulness

When you buy a new car, you have to consider what kind of driver you are and how you are going to use the car while you own it. If you are the kind of person who moves often, you will want a car that has some carrying capacity to get you from one apartment to the next. If you have to do a lot of tight parking in crowded spaces in the big city, a smaller car that handles easily will be a plus for you. If you perform in a rock-and-roll band and need to carry your amplifiers around, some sort of van is in order. If you sell real estate, you need a larger car that can carry a family around in comfort while you're selling them a house.

It's frustrating to spend a lot of money on a car, and then have to borrow someone else's to accomplish what you need to do regularly. So consider the matter carefully before you buy. This is tough because you may have two different life-style images tugging at you as you buy a car. If you're a real estate salesperson who would really love to have a sports car, you've just got to sell more houses so you can afford two cars.

Style and Color

Sometimes people tell me they don't care about the shape of a car, how it looks, or what color it is. I suppose there's no reason why it should matter—it's something you're certainly free to ignore. But you should know that your car, like your clothes, does *say* something about you. People judge you by your car (although you, of course, are free to ignore them). Remember how in high school a girl would check out a guy by the kind of car he had? Not all of us are that superficial, but something like that still goes on in adult life.

As you're shopping for a car, it's important to let yourself be open to new discovery. You might find yourself attracted to a particular style of car. If you thought you definitely wanted a white car, you might find yourself seduced by the baby blue. Just make sure that your new choice is something *you* want, and not something the salesman has hypnotically suggested.

Notice, too, how color can completely change the appearance of a car. A car that looks sporty in yellow can be very conservative in brown, and a car that looks understated in white can be quite flashy in red.

The color of a car can affect safety to a certain degree. Dark cars, of course—black and dark blue—are less visible at night. Gray and silver cars can blend in with the road, especially during the twilight hours when so many accidents occur. The color of a car can also affect its resale value. If you buy a color that you like, but that no one else likes, remember that it might take you longer to sell the car, or you might have to take a lower price when it comes time to get rid of it. Around the car lots that I've explored, silver, white, and red were the most popular colors. Another factor to consider is a color that doesn't show the dirt as easily, if you don't like to wash your car; that is why white is disliked by some people. They say red cars get more traffic tickets, but I don't know if that's because police notice red cars, or because the people who buy red cars drive faster. But buy the color you want, regardless of what anyone says. It's your car and you deserve at least that much for plunking down your money.

The style and color of a car are important, too, because they affect your mood in some subtle way. If you take the trouble to pick a car that you find more attractive, you'll find you're a lot more willing to take care of it, and you'll be happier driving it.

Comfort and Luxury

A lot of people don't appreciate the options available for a car's interior. They think of saving money, and even though they spend $7,000 on a car, they get the most basic, stripped-down model. You have the feeling you are sitting in the waiting room of a police station, when, for a few hundred dollars more, you could be riding in comfort, having a great time. Even little things, like an armrest, can transform the driving experience.

Now that you'll be saving so much money by being a sharp customer, you will certainly be able to afford a few extras to make things more comfortable. Like a cloth interior. A few people still prefer vinyl, based on the theory that it's easier to clean, but cloth seats, most people find, are preferable. They're cooler in summer and warmer in winter, and you don't have to worry about spilling things on them. Any dime store sells effective fabric cleaners that you can use if you do get them dirty.

Air conditioning is a nice thing, even if you only use it a few days a year. If you live in a place that gets very hot in the summer, have mercy on the friends who will ride in the car with you. However, air conditioning is expensive and also one of the things in the car most likely to need maintenance in the long run.

A good cassette radio can bring you close to paradise. But I strongly suggest you not buy any additional radio or tape deck from the dealer. Take whatever the *factory* put in the car, but don't submit to anything extra. There are a couple of reasons for this. Dealer car stereo systems are basically inferior, and they are overpriced for what they are. Every salesman I've ever met lies about this. *"You've got to listen to our gargantuan sound. It's the greatest sound system in a car, ever!"* Tell them you think it sounds like cats in an alley. A few of them are starting to sound decent, but they're wickedly overpriced.

If you really want sound that will knock your socks off, go to one of the car stereo specialty stores. Those guys are experts at installing equipment attractively in your car, and they will sell you superb sound for a lot less than you'll pay the dealer. *Never* buy extra music equipment from a dealer—it's just not worth the money. Car stereo stores will sell you some beautiful four-speaker systems for under $400.

My pet car fetish is the sunroof. It's only about $200–300 extra, and yet it can make you feel like a millionaire. Get one installed at the factory, if you can; they're less likely to leak. Most car dealers will install a sunroof for you, but it's usually better not to bother with the dealer. The dealer simply farms the work out to a sunroof shop, and adds a commission for himself. If you do use the dealer, the price on the sunroof is *very* negotiable. My recommendation is to call a few sunroof shops listed in the yellow pages, and get it done yourself. Get some referrals, if you can. Fly-by-night sunroof places do crummy work, and you'll find in the next rainstorm that the damn thing leaks.

Before you order a new sunroof, you should insist on seeing an example of the exact model you intend to buy. Take a good look, and use your common sense. Does the latch look cheap and likely to break? Will it leak? Don't listen to the salesman's babble about "guarantees"; trust your judgment.

In terms of an overall comfortable ride, American cars are hard to beat. I'm not sure anyone has devoted as much effort to comfortable suspensions as the American car manufacturers.

Inexpensive foreign cars and sports cars tend to give a hard ride. But even expensive imports, some drivers feel, don't have the soft suspensions of big American cars. Europeans and Japanese live in smaller countries where people don't drive as much as in America, and hence their cars have not always emphasized long-distance driving comfort. American car suspensions can be very comfortable: my Chrysler turbo coupe gives me the feeling of flying on a jet-powered living room sofa.

Handling and Performance

There really is a distinctive *feel* to each car, the way it takes a corner, the way it accelerates, the way it cruises down the open road. You and the machine become one at certain moments, and driving becomes a great aesthetic experience.

Okay, maybe not for you. But for some of us, that sweet feel behind the wheel is a big part of the car mystique. And for nearly everyone, there's something special about the feel of a new car. This is one of the salesman's big techniques for selling you. The salesman thinks that if he can just get you to drive that new car, he'll have you hooked. After all, almost any new car is better than the jalopy you drove into the showroom parking lot.

If you're going to spend a lot of time driving, you can make that driving time fun by having a car that is fun to drive. Since almost any new car is "nice" to drive in some way, you must learn to resist the salesman's pressure. Test drive enough cars to make an intelligent decision. The first new car you look at will probably be "nice," but somewhere out there may be a car that you'll find truly superb and perfect for you. If you think you have to check out cars X and Y and Z before you decide, don't be fooled by how nice X is when you drive it. Y and Z may be even better; if they're not, you'll at least know why X is the best car for you.

The performance/handling question is not decided by reading a magazine. You simply have to drive the cars in question. Thus, the absolute necessity in car shopping is a test drive, in more than one car, with a salesman who keeps his mouth shut so you can really *feel* the car. The better salesmen will know to stop talking while you drive so that the car can seduce you on its own. He'll begin his rap a little later on. The bad salesman will keep talking to you the whole time, and you may have to take strong measures. "You know, I might like to buy this car if only you'd shut up and let me drive it!"

When you're test driving a new car, feel free to "lean on it" a little bit. Turn corners quickly; accelerate fast; gun it enough so that the turbo kicks in. You've got to know *now* how it feels. There's no need to drive the car like a wimp. It's important for safety, too, that you know how quickly the engine responds, how swiftly the car brakes. The test drive is a time when you're absolutely in charge, so have fun putting this prospective new car of yours through its paces. Don't worry, the dealer is insured!

4

Understanding the
Auto-Sales Racket

When you walk into a new car showroom, you're in an uncertain environment. You're unsure about the cars, and you're unsure about how the car-buying process works. Your uncertainty is the salesman's best tool in robbing you of your money. Since you don't know what you're doing, the dealer is hoping you will rely on the "professional"—the car salesman—to guide you through the auto-buying process. After all, isn't that the smart thing to do—ask the "professional" in the field?

In "car school," where I learned how to be a car salesman, I was taught to be an authority figure in the showroom, to be both paternal and domineering while I tried to win the customer's trust. The dealer's hope is that your faith in the authority of the car salesman will lead you to sign on the dotted line for whatever the salesman asks. This works because unless you're lucky enough to know better, it's hard to say no to the salesman's lies. You are tempted to believe him when he says that there is no discount, that every intelligent person buys a car with this or that option, and so on.

But there is only one thing you need to be able to win the game against the salesman: correct information. By the time you're done reading this, you will be an experienced auto shopper. You will have heard the lies before.

The truth is that as a customer you always have the upper hand. You are playing a game that is definitely yours to win. The reason you have the upper hand is that you don't have to buy the car, and the salesman is desperate to sell it to you. If you don't buy the car, the salesman earns no commission, has nothing to show for the time he spends. The salesman can only have the upper hand if you don't understand the car-buying process or if you are psychologically vulnerable to his influence. But you should know that the final strength is with you. You don't have to buy the car, and so, no matter how smooth the salesman seems, he is actually squirming inside until that final moment when you decide to buy the car.

You have the upper hand even if you are buying a rare, hard-to-get car. Suppose you want to buy the only El Plusho convertible in the store. Maybe the manager will not be bargained down as much as on the easily available Hardride Sedan, but you will find that the salesman is still desperate to sell to *you*. Although the dealer may sell the car to someone else, the commission in that case will go to another salesman, and so you will still find the salesman working hard as long as he feels you are a serious buyer.

As an informed customer, you are in control. This is important, because buying a car is definitely a situation in which it pays to take the trouble to be on top of things. In many other areas, you often work with people you can trust. Although some doctors are quacks and thieves, it is likely that you know a good doctor. Although some lawyers are greedy and irresponsible, many lawyers are helpful, noble, ethical. But an honest car salesman is as rare as a four leaf clover. If a car salesman can profit by telling a lie, he probably will tell it. Oh sure, he may be friendly and helpful and even truthful when it doesn't affect his pocket—or when he is afraid he won't get away with a lie—but in that ultimate moment when your money is at stake, he will lie relentlessly. Like all good liars, he will mix his lies with the truth so that they seem more believable.

The Salesman and His Manager

When you buy a pair of socks, the department store trusts one person to carry through the sale from start to finish. The person in the sock department can recommend socks that are especially warm or comfortable or long lasting; he can tell you which colors are "in"; he'll give you the straightforward price on any pair of socks you choose; and he'll ring up your sale on the cash register and give you a bag in which to take home your purchase.

Car sales are different. The managers don't trust the salesman to handle his sale all by himself. If they left him to his own devices, he might be a nice guy and give you a good price on the car. Car dealers find they make a lot more money if the salesmen are under the control of a manager who guides them through every step of the negotiations. The manager has the final say on every deal; nothing is final until the manager signs the form.

What kind of person is an auto-sales manager? A person who is not only good at manipulating people, but who is also very good at teaching others how to manipulate people. In a high-volume urban car dealership, he makes $100,000 or more annually. Almost always, the sales manager can think of some new lie to tell a customer when the salesman runs out of things to say. Sometimes a manager will come down from his perch to talk to a hostile, screaming customer, calm him down, and then sell him a car. In a very real sense he earns his high salary: he leads a platoon of salespeople in manipulating extra thousands of dollars from each of hundreds of customers.

You'll usually find the manager to be visible from the showroom floor, often on a raised, enclosed platform ("the cage" or "the tower") or in a big, separate office to the side of the floor. You can see managers whispering directions to salesmen who are hard at work trying to take somebody's money. When it is your turn to buy a car, they will whisper about you. It's rather flattering, and you will enjoy the attention. After all, how often do a group of people in the $100,000 salary range get together to have a talk about you, your needs, how to make you happy? When you're buying a car, the salesman, the manager, and anybody else on the dealer staff who happens to be there joins in a huddle to discuss: What kind of person are you? How easily can you be fooled? What kind of lies will you believe? Knowing that this is going on makes it easy for you to resist the lies that they will produce.

But why do they have two people work together? Isn't one liar enough? No, not really. Car salesmen may be liars, but they're human, too. A lot of them are all torn up inside about their desire to be decent human beings, on the one hand, and their desire to make a lot of money, on the other. Any person left on his own to tell lies to customers would be prone to give in and start giving better discounts.

Part of it is just that two heads are better than one. If you have two people thinking of lies to tell, two people to conspire to fool somebody, the tricks are likely to be a lot more successful.

Another reason for having two liars working together is that one of them—the salesman—can pretend to be your friend, and the salesman and his manager can work on you with the good guy/bad guy routine. The salesman can pretend to want to give you a good discount on a car: *"Hey, I wish I could sell you the car for that price. But that jerk the manager won't let me! I'll try my best, though! You know I'm working hard for you, don't you?"* As one manager said to his sales staff, "As far as you clowns are concerned, we're like the gods on Mount Olympus. You don't know what we'll do. You've got to act like you're working hard to get the customer a great deal."

The sales manager provides the dealer with a way of controlling salespeople. As one sales manager explained to me, "When you're the salesman, you get too emotionally involved in the deal. You're anxious to sell a car; plus you like the customer and want to give him a car at a good price. I'm here to see that you don't do that. If you want to give the customer too much of a discount, I'll say, "Whoa! Wait a minute! Tell him this," and half the time he'll believe it and there will be a lot more money in your pocket as well as in the dealership's."

We all need positive reinforcement. Even if you're a crooked car salesman, you need someone to respect you for what you're doing. If you're just a salesman working alone, lying to customers all day, it's easy to get depressed. You feel lonely and despicable. As a car salesman, though, you have your manager as well as your fellow salesmen for support, people with whom you can laugh at the gullibility of the public. The manager respects you for being tough, for telling lies successfully. He tells you what a good job you're doing. What's more, the manager helps you make money. Every time he tells you a lie that works with a customer or gives you some strategy on how to cheat a customer, it's extra money in your pocket since, as a salesman, you get about one-third of all the money you can steal. The manager is the one who guides you toward that $1,000 commission for a single car. Salesmen become devoted to their managers— there is good reason for using this two-person system!

At many modern car dealerships the salesman is in deep trouble unless he "TOs" the customer. "TO" refers to the practice of "turning" the customer "over" to the manager before the customer is allowed to leave. The salesman halts the customer—"Wait right there, sir!" —and quickly summarizes for the manager why he has failed to sell a car. The manager will suggest some new lie or approach to use or will deal with the customer himself. The TO system sharpens the wits of the salesmen by forcing them to explain each encounter to the manager and benefit from the manager's concrete advice, *and* it gives the dealer a second chance with each customer. If you are trying to leave a car dealer, and the salesman says, "Just a moment, ma'am, let me check something for you. I'll be back in a minute!" you'll know you are being TO'd.

Most customers don't get an opportunity to meet the manager. But when you show yourself to be a tough customer who doesn't buy the lies you hear, the manager will often try his charm on you personally. It's actually a funny experience. The manager is often Mr. Suave, qui-

etly impressing you with the fact that you are so important a customer that he has come down from Mount
Olympus to talk things over with you personally. Sometimes the salesman and his manager will talk to you
together, "working" you, as they say in the trade. Don't
worry, just enjoy the attention because you've got everything you need to know. But if you feel uncomfortable
and object to the two-person attack, just insist that you
want to talk to only one person at a time. They will
listen—you're the boss.

Selling You the Wrong Car, Today

A salesman's techniques for cheating you out of your
money are important to recognize, but don't overlook
the salesman's first and foremost job: to convince you to
buy a car, today. Even before he can think of charging
you too much for the car, or selling you services you
don't need, he has to convince you to buy a car.

There's nothing necessarily bad about this. A salesman's job is, after all, to make sales, and in any honest
business, it's perfectly all right for a salesman to spend
his best efforts in getting you comfortable with buying
the product.

For your part, though, it's important to understand the
pressures on the salesman both to sell you a car and to
sell you the wrong car. A lot of people get nailed by car
dealers because they start their car search by stopping in
at a dealer to "just go looking." By the time they visit
the second or third dealer, but often at the first one, they
meet a salesman who is good enough to put them in a car
and send them home.

Many of us go window shopping often, so why isn't it
safe to do the same with cars? Why can't we just look
without becoming victims of the salesman? Part of it is
that car salesmen are simply better salespeople. A business that can pay its salesmen $80,000 a year or more will
obviously attract some first-rate hustlers. "Just looking"
for a car is also more dangerous because we Americans

are a nation of impulse buyers. On how many afternoons have you gone out just looking and come back with new clothing or some knickknack for the living room? We do it very often, but blowing 20 bucks on impulse at a clothing store is a lot different from blowing 10,000 on an impulse purchase of a car. The scale of money is different, but the psychology is the same. We don't buy a car as often as we buy a new piece of clothing, but basically we are still kids out looking at new toys, whether in the jewelry shop or at a car dealer, and as long as the money is in our pockets we are just as vulnerable to spending it. Part of all this, too, is that cars are very wonderful toys, and it is easy for us to get seduced by the shiny newness of a dream on wheels. Part of it, too, is that large sums of money seem unreal. Twelve thousand five hundred and eighty-two dollars is an unreal number, more or less like the national debt. *"Well, sir, your payment of $238 per month is just a little more than 33 cents an hour. Is 33 cents too much to pay for a lovely car like this?"*

Car sales is not low pressure; it is high pressure, as you can clearly see when you understand the salesman's point of view. He sees maybe two customers a day, and will wind up spending an hour or perhaps even three or four with you. That's a lot of time, both in waiting for you and dealing with you, for a salesman not to be serious about making a sale. He can make nothing off you, or he can make a thousand dollars—another understandable incentive to give it his best shot. Most customers don't really get a second chance, either. If a salesman doesn't sell a customer on the spot, the customer disappears into the "be back hole." "We'll be back!" the customers lie as they leave. Nearly all of them don't come back. They buy a car from a salesman who is sharper.

When you drive up to a car dealer, especially if it isn't a busy day, you can see the sales staff hanging around, like vultures. As you walk up to the showroom, they form a quick image of you, based on your appearance and the car you brought with you. They make a few comments about you, until one of them decides to take the plunge, to begin the possibly three-hour effort to earn himself $1,000 based on your ignorance about how to buy a car.

If there's a rule that works for successful car salesmen, it's this: keep talking and say *anything* that will keep the customer with you until he buys a car *today*. The salesman has promised himself never to let a customer go without a struggle. The point is to convince the customer that there is some special deal, a once-in-a-lifetime discount or opportunity that the customer will profit from only if he or she buys a car *today*.

For your part, you get the salesman's hard work and attention if you fib and tell him that you are indeed willing to buy a car today, even if you're not. The salesman will put out his best efforts to get you accurate information and a good price only if he is convinced that you are a serious buyer, so play along with him.

The salesman is only successful in selling you a car today, of course, if he has a car he can convince you to buy. Thus he works to convince you that a car he has—or can get for you—is the right car even if it is the wrong car for you. After all, if the car that you've decided on is at a dealer down the road, then the salesman won't make any money.

Obviously, if a salesman sells Buicks, then his job is to convince you that a Buick—some Buick in his lot—is right for you. It may be that what you really want and need is a Buick, but you can't count on the salesman to be of any help in finding that out. Each of us is impressionable, and when you're face-to-face with a salesman, there's something inside of you that tugs at your heart. You find yourself trying to make the salesman happy! Almost any new car looks pretty nice when you first see it, and so it can seem like a good idea to buy it—that is, until you see a better car later on, a car that you realize you should have bought.

The salesman has to sell you on his inventory. If you want a two-door Tempo and the dealer only has four-door Tempos, you will be told numerous reasons why a four-door is really better.

There is a big push on salesmen to sell you one of the cars that the dealer has in stock. Part of the reasoning here is that the dealer will be more at ease if he can put you in a new car on the spot. If he needs to special-order a car for you, then it may not be easy to seduce you into signing papers for something you haven't seen.

Another reason the dealer wants to sell you something in stock is that he makes more money that way. Car dealers essentially "rent" their new cars from the manufacturer. Each day a car on the lot remains unsold, the dealer must pay interest on the car. The quicker he gets rid of it, the quicker the cash is in his hand. Better to sell something in stock that might have been gathering dust for a few weeks or months than to sell something that will be delivered in the future. Special-ordering from the factory is avoided whenever possible, because it takes a long time to get the car (longer than the dealer will admit to you) and sometimes a car is hard to get in the exact configuration the customer wants.

If you really want a car that has options X and Z but not Y, and the dealer does not have your exact car in stock, and hasn't been able to sell you one of the cars he has, he will very likely offer to "DX" a car for you. "DX" refers to "dealer exchange," meaning that the car dealer will call up the car you want on the computer and see what other dealer in the area has it. He will consider this to be a pain in the neck, because the salesman and some friend of his will have to drive out there to pick it up. In addition to this wasted time, he will have to pay the other dealer at least $400 for the privilege of taking his car out of his inventory. The $400-plus comes out of the profit margin, which directly reduces the price reduction you can negotiate for yourself. Unless your time is so valuable that you can afford to lose $400, it is better to drive around to different dealers yourself to find the car you want.

(A Customer's Sneaky Trick: If the car salesman offers to find you the car you want at another dealer, tell him to go ahead and run the computer. When he comes back with the printout, start asking him a lot of dumb questions about interior colors and other options, so he will keep looking at the printout. During your questioning, see if you can't peek at the printout and find the name of the dealer that has the car you want. Act undecided, leave, go to the other dealer, and buy the car!)

The salesmen have special incentives to sell certain undesirable cars to customers. If a car's been on the lot a long time, or if it's had a lot of mechanical problems (despite being new) or arrived at the dealer wrecked, or if it's a lemon, or a demonstrator with a ridiculous number of miles on it, the dealer will sometimes give a bonus commission (often $100 to $200) to the salesman who sells that car. A salesman's attempt to steer you toward a particular car is usually the signal that he's hoping to make some special bonus from selling that car, and you should be especially careful about inspecting such a car before you buy it.

The salesman will try hard to sell you the wrong car because it is one of *his* cars. As a smart customer, however, you will take a good look at cars on the street, and at friends' cars, before you go shopping. You will also be visiting several dealers to look at cars and thus be making a great many salesmen miserable when it turns out you don't buy a car from them. Don't feel guilty, though; they know it's a tough business, and they're making plenty of money.

I Know a Car Salesman—He'll Give Me a Great Deal!

Car salesmen take special advantage of friends and even cheat their own relatives, so beware! If your cousin or brother-in-law or neighbor is a car salesman, I guarantee he'll be very friendly when you walk into his dealership. You will very likely be offered a small-to-middling discount that will be represented to you as a "great deal." But you rarely get the kind of discount a sharp customer gets. *"Come on, he lives on my block! He wouldn't give me a bum deal."*

It's important not to be misled by a salesman's friendliness. An effective salesman is friendly with all of his customers, and he has learned that you can be friendly while still charging people $2,000 more than they have to pay for a car. Much of a salesman's business comes from neighbors, friends, and relatives. The commission structure is such that if he gives all these people a *truly* good deal, he'll severely limit his own income. Why bother to give people a really good deal, when instead you can just convince them they're getting a good deal and still keep a good profit in your own pocket?

It might be better to buy a car from a stranger, so you won't feel guilty about pounding on him about the price. Or go shop at your friend's dealer. Joke and laugh with your car-salesman neighbor or cousin while you push him down to a good price. Treat it like a game, and watch him laugh, too, while he sweats underneath his suit.

One manager admitted that he even overcharged his own mother. "Oh, I'm not denying I gave her a discount," he said. "She got a discount, sure. But there was still a good profit for me. I work for a living, after all, and she's got Social Security. You know, she drove away with a smile, and even sent me another customer two weeks later. Like I always say, a good deal is in the mind of the customer!"

5

Ways of Stealing Your Money

The Lie That There Is No Discount

The lies salesmen tell are really amazing. Chances are a salesman will look you right in the eye and calmly say, "I'm sorry, but there's no discount on new models. We do have discounts on a few demonstrators from last year, but the new models sell at full price." Go ahead and laugh. The salesman's theory is that it never hurts to try. Even if five out of ten customers laugh in his face, three of the others will consider it seriously for a while and the other two will believe him and write a check.

In the last few years, the lie that there is no discount has been especially popular with the guys who sell the popular Japanese cars, Toyotas and Hondas and Nissans. *These Toyotas are selling like hotcakes! There ain't no discount!* Makes sense, doesn't it? Plus they seem so sincere! They will try to bluff you out on this one, even insisting on it several times—but there's almost always a discount. You just gotta keep pulling, trying it at a couple of dealers, if necessary, keep hammering until they give you one. Tell them you don't feel comfortable buying a car without a discount. The salesman wants his commission, and he'll get around to offering a discount so that he can make his money. Remember, even if Hondas are in great demand, the dealer has jacked up his price even higher just in the hope that some fool will pay it.

The Lie That a Small Discount Is His Rock-Bottom Price

Most car buyers get some kind of discount. Word is out that you should get a discount when you buy a car, although most customers don't know how much. "Wow! I got $300 off!" Yes, $300 does buy a lot of jelly beans. But before you get overly impressed at the dealer's generosity, you must think about the possibility that you should be getting $1,300 or even more off the sticker price of the car. In the following chapters, I'll show you how to calculate what the real discount on a car should be. How odd it is that in this one area, where the salesman has so much incentive to lie, the customer trusts the very same salesman to tell him the truth! You might feel you got a good deal because you argued for two hours, because the salesman moaned and groaned about how he's not making any money, because the manager complimented you on what a hard bargainer you are. Beware! A small discount is not a great triumph at a car dealer.

The Lie That There Is a Special Deal *Today*

This is a favorite tactic of the auto-sales racket. Salesmen love to create the false excitement that will lead you to buy a car from them right now. *"Hey, the manager's going out of his mind today!* (Managers never mind if the salesmen insult them—if it will help sell a car.) *He's offering you this incredible $500 discount if you'll buy the car right now. There's no way this offer is going to be there tomorrow. So if you'll just autograph the paperwork, we'll have you rolling home with a great car and a great deal!"*

There is never, ever such a thing as a special price today that won't be good tomorrow, except on the special occasions when the *manufacturer* (not the dealer!) is offering a rebate/financing incentive. A good car-deal negotiator—someone like you—can get the same good price anytime, anywhere. The same good deal—or a better one—can be had tomorrow at the same dealer or at another one down the road.

The idea of the special deal that is good only *today* is one of the greatest and most successful lies in the kingdom of car dealers. It is a powerful lie, because as a customer you think, "Gosh, what if this is true? I don't want to be dumb enough to pass up a great deal." Add to this your natural wish to wrap up a deal quickly, and you can see why this lie works.

Car sales is too much of a bottom-line business. It's basically always the same. There's no such thing as a "sale": "$1,000 off! Guaranteed $1,000 on your trade-in! Free rustproofing! Free round-trip ticket to Paris!" Or whatever. With a profit margin of several thousand dollars on each car, the dealer can always afford to take a portion of the profit margin and offer it to the public as a sale price, free gift, discount coupon, or whatever else will succeed in teasing you.

Your Choice: Money in Your Pocket or the Dealer's

Once you've settled on a car, you begin a battle with the salesman. Most of the time, when you decide you want a product, you tell the clerk, he wraps it up, you take it home.

But buying a car is different. You decide you want a car, but before you drive it away, there is a lengthy session ahead. You will have to peel away lie after lie of the salesman's presentation. There is the value of the car, for which you must pay, and a certain reasonable profit to the dealership: there is no argument about that. But then there is this extra amount of money, as much as $4,000, which will become the cause of a battle between you, on the one hand, and the salesman and other dealer employees, on the other. The salesman gets up to one-third of the extra money he can extract from your pocket. How much extra do you want to give this bunch of liars? I say nothing is what they deserve, beyond the reasonable profit already included in a good minimum-gross deal. After all, they lie so much, and they're so rich from cheating other people, why should we give these clowns an extra penny? Even if you're rich, there are charities much more deserving of your money than a crooked crew of people at a car dealership.

When you think about it in this light, you will find that your inner resolve strengthens. They're trying to cheat you out of some of your hard-earned money. For your own dignity, you shouldn't let them do it. You don't have to sign the papers until the deal is perfect.

They'll Cheat You on the Value of Your Trade-in

It's a great American tradition to trade in your car at a car dealer. It's certainly convenient. You drop off the old battlewagon and go home in your shiny new chariot of metal and chrome. The problem is that it is easy to lose lots of money on a trade-in. Lots of money. A trade-in can double the dealer's opportunity to make a profit off of you.

Car salesmen love it when you say you have a trade-in. They feel it gives them an extra edge in tricking you out of your money. It's one more thing with which to confuse you—your emotions about your old car are a weapon to be used against you in the overall price battle. Salesmen are trained to ask you a lot of questions about your old car in order to determine your feelings about it. They are also trained to go over your trade-in's bad points, slowly, so that it's diminished value can sink in.

When they appraise the value of your old car, the figure they come up with is a secret that will not be revealed to you. The salesman and his manager may play the game either of two ways. Most likely, they will seriously undervalue the wholesale cost of your trade-in. If you hate your old car, the salesman will be happy to confirm that hate with a low offer. Otherwise, you will be given 50 reasons why your old car is not worth as much as you think it is.

If you're really attached to your old car, the salespeople may use another tactic. They may offer you more than your car is worth. "Wow! They gave me $1,000 for my old rustbucket!" They'll even do that for a car worth $50. How? Of course, they simply take the other $950 out of the profit margin on the new car. Offering you too much for your trade-in is a very effective way for a salesman to press the hot button that will induce you to buy a new car, today.

With your trade-in, the dealer now has another opportunity to cheat you. In addition to preventing you from getting the discount on your new car, the salesman will work hard, in most cases, to prevent you from getting the full wholesale value on your old car, too. He also gets a commission on the difference between what you *accept* on the old car and its *real* value.

Now, when you trade in your car at a dealer, the best you can expect—after hard bargaining—is a solid wholesale offer on your car, except when the dealer teases you by offering too much for the old car, and thus reducing or eliminating the discount on the new one. By "wholesale," I mean the price that a dealer will pay you for a car that he will sell to someone else at a higher, "retail" price, usually at least $500 more. Wholesale is less than retail because of the need for the dealer to make some profit when he resells the car.

What happens to your used car after you trade it in to the dealer? One of two things. The dealer will keep the better used cars for his own used car lot, and he will sell or rewholesale the rest, with a small profit over what he paid to you, to a used car dealer or auto broker, a middleman who will resell it to another dealer. When a dealer sells a used car to a customer, he plays the same discount games as with a new car. If the dealer pays you $4,500 for your trade-in, he may put it on lot with an asking price of $6,500, though he would accept an actual retail price of $5,200 from a sharp customer.

You can make more money by selling the car yourself, privately, but this isn't always easy. Using the guidebooks to used car prices ("Bibles," the salesmen call them) is not always helpful, since there are so many variables in the condition of each car. The best way to find out how much your old car is worth is to shop it, that is, take it around for estimates to several dealers and see what they will offer for it. Try both a couple of used car dealers and two used car departments in new car dealers. The best of these offers is your wholesale price. If you can sell it privately, through an ad in the newspaper or a sign in the laundromat, you'll usually get a higher price, provided you aren't pressured to sell it quickly. People will expect to get a bargain from you, less than they would pay a used car dealer at retail, but you can expect to sell it for a couple hundred more than wholesale, what a car dealer would pay you for the car. Many people like to buy a car from its owner, since they know you'll feel guilty if you hide the car's problems from the new purchaser. Besides, most people would pay too high a price at a car dealer for a used car, so it's a real bargain to buy it from an individual at a little above wholesale.

One of the more outrageous scams on trade-ins is the "100 percent sale," in which a dealer promises to give you 100 percent of the original purchase price of your used car, if that car is three years old or less, as a trade-in allowance on a new car. The catch is that you would indeed get 100 percent of its original price, but *minus* any "necessary" (ha!) repairs. The "necessary" repairs are billed at crazy prices: the car always has to be repainted, at a cost of $1900, and so on. People wind up getting pitifully little for their trades, but the scam works! The customers who were cheated walked away happy, saying, "Hey! I got 100% of the price of my old car back . . ."

Charging Too Much for Financing

A lot of the profits at a car dealer are not "front end" profits, i.e., profits on the price of the car itself, but rather "back end" profits, i.e., profits obtained from the services and paperwork that have become part of the modern car transaction. High on the list of things to loathe in the auto racket is the finance operation. Here's why the finance manager is so highly paid.

It's so convenient to finance at the car dealer, isn't it?

You just go into the back office, the finance man puts the numbers in the computer, and the machine spits it out. You sign, and it's all done. You go home, without having to mess around with banks. Isn't it nice?

No, not really. The finance manager is a highly paid master of deceit. People lose thousands in the finance office of the dealership. The finance guy has to be good at numbers *and* good at bamboozling people. Often he succeeds at cheating people where the salesman has failed. You've dickered with the salesman about a price; you're tired, drained, exhausted, and the finance guy will just slide the stuff right by you. You'll sign, and only realize much later how badly you were taken.

When you're shopping for a car, the salesmen will swear up and down that their financing is "as competitive as any bank." After all, a big company like Ford or GM or Honda can get loan money a lot cheaper than you can, and so they can give it to you at the best interest rate, right? In a sense this is true; they can give you money at a good interest rate, but they *won't* unless you squeeze it out of them.

The finance guy gets a commission from whatever extra interest he can squeeze out of you. If the going rate for car loans is 12 percent, the finance guy will offer you a loan somewhere between 14 and 19 percent, most likely, and he will pocket a share of the extra money you will be paying in interest over the next three or four years. Often it is purely up to him to decide how much interest to charge you. If you seem educated, sophisticated, confident of your credit, he will charge you 14 percent. If you seem unsure of your credit, uneducated, or confused, he may charge you 18 or 19 percent, up to the highest rate allowed by law, and hope he will get away with it.

He will back up his statement with a bunch of lies, to the effect that the interest rate listed is "standard" for car loans. If you don't buy that, he will tell you that your bank will have extra hidden costs that will actually make it cost more than dealer financing. He will tell you of various advantages that come from using Chrysler Credit or whatever. If he tried to sell you interest at 19 percent, and you didn't buy it, you'll find yourself bargaining all over again: he'll go down to 17 percent, talk with the manager, and go down to 16 percent. If you refuse at 14 percent when the bank rate is 12 percent, he may tell you to go to your bank because the profit margin for him is getting too small for him to bother.

Even if you feel that your credit is pretty bad, you shouldn't let a finance manager push outrageous interest on you. Tell him you won't take the car home unless he can work out a satisfactory rate of interest, not more than one point above the going bank rate. He'll respect you more and even think of you as a better credit risk if you're a hard bargainer. For many folks, however, it's much easier and more economical to get a loan through the local bank or credit union.

Even if you are getting a car loan through a bank or credit union, it still pays to shop around. At any time you can find a spread of two interest points or more on car loans. You might think you'll get a loan more easily with your own bank, but it never hurts to apply to a few others. You can often apply for the loan before you go to the car dealer, to be sure you've got a loan approved in a certain amount before you go car shopping.

If you do provide your own financing, you will still have to deal with the finance man at the car dealer. The finance man will take your down payment and arrange for the final paperwork on the deal. He'll get the check from your bank when it's ready. He'll give you the car to take home on a "ten-day note" or something similar, i.e., you have ten days to come up with the rest of the money on your car, allowing time for your bank loan to go through.

The Trick of Offering Low Financing

What about all this "8.8 percent financing" you hear about? Is it real? How can dealers offer financing at 4 or 8 percent at times when even large corporations have to borrow money at 11 percent? Sometimes such low financing is real. Most of the time, however, there is a trick to it, and the customer may even lose money because of the "low" financing rate! How so? In a nutshell, when you get a low financing rate, you usually pay a lot more for the car—so you may end up spending just as much money or more despite the low interest.

Car dealers know that most customers don't know the difference between a good deal and a bad deal. There are so many different types of cars, and so many different versions of the same car, that a customer has only a vague idea about what is a good price for a particular car. What almost every person *does* understand is the difference between high and low interest rates: we all appreciate that a loan at 10 percent is better than a loan at 12 percent.

When your bank is giving car loans at, say, 12 percent, it seems like a miracle when the dealer offers you a car loan at 8 percent (wow!) or 4 percent (double wow!) or even 0 percent (triple wow and I can't believe it!). The auto business knows that it is very provocative to offer these low loan rates. Salesmen know from experience that a customer will pay $3,000 more for a car, and will jump at the chance to buy a car today, if he or she gets the chance to say, "Wowee, I got a loan at 4 percent interest!" When I tell people I paid $10,900 for my last car, most people don't know that it was a good price or that other folks paid $4,000 more for the identical car. But if I would say, "Hey, I got a car loan at 6 percent interest," the immediate response is, "Wow, man, you got a great deal!"

The dealer, or the manufacturer, gives you a low interest loan by using some of his cash—some of his profit margin on the car—and using that cash to "buy down" the interest rate. For example, let's say that the bank rate on car loans—the real cost of loan money—is 14 percent. Now examine this table:

Amount financed

(Five-year loan)	Interest rate	Monthly payment
$10,000	14%	$232.69
$10,500	12%	$233.58
$11,000	10%	$233.73

Suppose Joe Salesman walks up to you and says, "You know, if you buy this $11,000 car and buy it right now, I'll get you a 10 percent car loan—that's *four full points* below the bank interest rate! But you better buy it now!" You might think you're being offered a great deal. But notice that if you get $1,000 off the price but pay the full 14 percent interest rate, you actually get a better deal!

Notice how, as the interest rate goes *down,* your monthly payment goes *up* when you pay just a little more on the price of the car. Many customers don't understand how to get a discount on the price of a car; they do, however, notice the interest-rate figure, which makes it easy for a car dealer to "buy down" the loan rate by just making sure the customer pays full price, or close to full price, on a new car. When the factory sticker price has add-ons for "additional dealer markup," "required rustproofing," and so on, the dealer has a nice fat profit margin that allows him to play games with the interest rate if he senses that a low one will make you happy.

A "low interest rate" that is advertised by the *dealer* (and not the manufacturer) is pointless. The dealer simply will charge you closer to his full asking price to pay for the lower interest rate. You'll be just as well off, or even better (because the calculations are easier) to take your full discount on the car price and pay the going loan rate as advertised by major banks.

Sometimes, but only sometimes, you *can* get a good deal when the low interest rate is offered by the *manufacturer* (and not by the dealer). In other words, the car company itself, Chrysler or American Motors or whoever, is really giving a discount by paying for cheap interest rates. As a smart customer, you can get a good deal if you get the proper discount on the car price from the dealer *and* get the low interest rate offered by the manufacturer. But this "if" is where most customers lose. Customers are usually so happy to get a low interest rate on their loans that they pay full price, or close to full price, for the car. When the auto industry is running its interest rate "specials," sales go up. When sales go up, the cars are hotter, more in demand, and thus you must work harder to get a good discount from the dealer. The dealer profits more when the manufacturer pays for low interest rates, while you, the customer, might be no better off than before.

The advertising of low finance rates has other tricks, too. Sometimes, the super-low rate (2.5 percent!) has conditions that most customers cannot meet, such as; (a) you need at least $3,000 in cash as a down payment; (b) the rate only applies to two-year car loans with monthly payments in excess of $400 per month. If you are the more average customer with maybe $1,000 in cash and you want a five-year car loan with monthly payments under $300, you'll find you have to pay a higher interest rate close to the bank rate.

The auto business discovered in the mid-1980s that low interest rates are very exciting to customers. Manufacturers and dealers are raising the prices of cars generally to pay for such low financing. In Britain, automakers quite regularly sell cars at zero interest rates; of course, the price of the car already includes enough profit to cover the cost of the so-called interest free car loan. America is tending toward a similar system as customers get used to being able to brag about low-interest and no-interest car loans. What was originally a quick sales gimmick for slow periods may become an institution, as new car prices include sufficient profits to pay for low loan rates.

In summary, there is no real reason to get excited about low interest rates. What you save in this one area, you usually pay for in another. The low loan rates can be an advantage when they are sponsored by the manufacturer, not the dealer, but in such cases: (1) the dealer will try to use your excitement about the loan rate to get you to pay full price for the car; (2) restrictive conditions may apply; and (3) the overall savings is usually not big enough to justify buying a car before you're ready.

Low interest rates sponsored by the manufacturer may indeed save you from $200 to $1,000 on your overall cost. But that is less than the other savings you will get from reading this book, and it is not a sufficient incentive to buy the wrong car at the wrong time. Furthermore, savings from a low loan rate may not be as much as the cash discount usually offered as an alternative. If GM is offering "8.8 percent financing" or "$750 off," you might be better off with the cash discount.

The same warnings that apply to "discount coupons" apply to "low financing rates." Discount coupons supplied by a dealer are virtually meaningless, relative to the amount you can save by negotiating the car's price on your own; discount coupons supplied by the manufacturer should not hinder you from getting your full discount from the dealer.

Bogus Extras That Cost Thousands

Although car dealers make a lot of money by not giving you the discount you deserve on the price of the car, they can make even more by selling you a bunch of bogus extras, unneeded products, and services that add thousands to the price of your car. These profit scams are amazingly successful. The sales managers I know regularly marvel that these scams work as well as they do. If you ever look at the auto-trade magazines, the ones that dealers read, you will find shameless ads from companies that will show car dealers how to increase their profit margins by selling these bogus services and defeating customer resistance to them.

Your best rule is: Say no to *everything*.

On almost any new car purchase, you can lose $2,000 or more to these scams. Traditionally, many of these scams were "after-market," sold to you after you had agreed to buy the car. The more advanced technique involves selling these on the car itself, on a second, "add-on" sticker next to the regular factory sticker on the car. This helps give the impression that you can't turn these products or services down, that they've already been applied to the car in some way, that it is a standard part of the price you pay for the car, that it's something you can't negotiate or can only reduce rather than eliminate. The second-sticker routine has been one of the most successful moneymakers ever invented by the auto-sales industry, a fraud scheme that has been remarkable in making millions for dealers with relatively little resistance by the public.

There is nothing you should buy from the car dealer other than the car itself. Nothing on the add-on sticker, no extras salesmen try and sell you, nothing! It's just about all garbage; anything really worth getting can be gotten better and cheaper somewhere else.

The extras are viewed as almost pure profit by the dealership. This means that you can refuse or negotiate away all the extras if they are listed on the add-on sticker. When you negotiate the price of a car, just look at the add-on sticker as so much baloney—that's the way the sales manager looks at it! You're shooting for a figure well *below* the *factory* sticker, and thus way below the add-on sticker.

When you buy a car, you should be buying the car, period. Say no to everything extra, and watch how many thousands of dollars you save. Depending on the dealer, these extras will be sold in one or more of four different ways:

1. Some of the extras may be sold on the add-on sticker, as if they were already a part of the new car price.
2. Some may be sold by the car salesman himself.
3. Some may be sold by a special staff member whose only job is to give the pitch about rustproofing, extended service contracts, etc.
4. Some will be sold to you by the wily finance manager.

The popular scams involving extras are listed below.

Extras to Avoid

Rustproofing
Undercoating
Glaze
Fabric protection
Dealer-installed equipment
Preparation charges
Processing fees
Extended service contracts
Credit life insurance
Accident, health, and disability insurance
Anything else they think of

The Great Rustproofing and Undercoating Hoax

"How long do you plan to keep your new car?"

"Oh, about three or four years."

"And then you plan to sell it?"

"I suppose so."

"So the resale value of your car is important to you, isn't it?"

"Oh, sure."

"You know, rustproofing helps preserve your car against the natural effects of weather; it stops the deterioration that would normally happen to a car. A car that's not rusted out is more valuable, isn't it?"

"Oh, sure."

"So you see, if you get your car rustproofed now, which is on special this month for only $695, you'll more than recover that amount of money in the resale value of your car. Isn't that a good bargain?"

One of the great marvels of the auto business is that the whole rustproofing scam still works. Rustproofing—it sounds like such a good thing to get, such an intelligent precaution to take for your car. Yet it's one of the most shameless frauds of the whole auto-sales racket.

Why is it a fraud? Isn't preventing rust a good thing?

First of all, modern cars are rustproofed at the factory. Sometimes, the sales brochures even show the galvanized body panels being prepared against the dangers of rust. There is really no need to get anything extra.

Second, many dealers do *nothing* to your car even though they charge you for rustproofing. After all, how would you tell? If something is actually done, it is often a mere whiz of rustproofing solution over some obvious spots. In either case it is virtually cost-free to the dealer. A thorough job of rerustproofing your car is almost unheard of.

Third, the dealer management looks at the rustproofing charge as pure profit; they laugh at any customer who swallows this bait. Salesmen are trained to brag about what a great thing it is, but every salesman knows it's a fraud.

Fourth, if you really want your car rerustproofed for

dealing with the Vermont winter or whatever, rustproofing will be accomplished more thoroughly and cheaply ($100 to $200) by private rustproofing companies, listed in the yellow pages under "Automotive Services" or even "Rustproofing."

The same goes for the mythical "undercoating," which some car dealers charge you for as a separate service.

Glaze and Fabric Protection

Glaze—an extra coat of wax. Fabric protection—a can of a Scotch Guard–type substance whizzed over the seats. Sometimes you pay hundreds of dollars for this stuff! Don't believe a word of whatever you hear about this junk. Most of the time nothing at all is done to the car, because, once again, how would you tell? It is purely profit, a complete fraud. When a dealer tries to sell you these extras, it's an appropriate time to contemplate the depravity of humankind.

Dealer-installed Equipment

Nearly every new car you buy has options, of course. The Washington, D.C., area where I live, has a long, hot summer, so nearly every car on a dealer's lot has air conditioning. Most options, however, are put on the car at the factory at the same time that the car is built. You can tell because the options and their prices are listed on the original factory sticker. The total price listed on the factory sticker is already negotiable; it includes a minimum profit for the dealer, plus a great deal of extra profit from a customer who doesn't realize that he has the right to question that price.

A dealer increases his profit margin, by adding some other options onto the car right at the dealership or by contract with an independent supplier. Two of the popular options installed by dealers are sunroofs and pinstripes.

Now, I'm a big fan of sunroofs, as I mentioned previously. A car with a good sunroof is definitely worth a little extra money. If you can't get a factory sunroof, it's going to cost something to pay a guy to saw a hole in the roof and make sure the cover doesn't leak. I like pinstripes, too. They can make a car look especially attractive. If you like pinstripes on the car, feel free to indulge yourself.

The problem with both these options is price. It's more than the fact that, with another option, the dealer has an extra chance to make a profit. With a dealer-installed option, the dealer has a chance to make an outrageous profit, especially if you believe the price he charges for it.

Pinstripes will often cost you $125 or more as listed on the dealer's add-on sticker. How much are they really worth? Two bucks for the striped tape and five minutes for the prep guy to put them on. Why does the dealer charge so much? He hopes he'll be lucky and that you'll pay the price he quotes. He also figures that even if you bargain him down a little from his original high price, he's still got a tremendous profit after the negotiations are complete.

If you want something added to your car at the dealer—a cassette deck, or body side moldings to protect your car from damage—the salesman will often pull a price out of thin air. After all, no harm in going for the gusto, is there? If it hasn't been done to the car already, better to get it done afterward, from an independent (and less expensive) contractor.

If you don't like the dealer-installed options—let's say you hate sunroofs—then go find a car without them. But if you do like them, you don't have to turn them down just because the price is outrageous. Just negotiate the price of that option down to a more reasonable level. Remember, the percentage of markup in a dealer-installed option can be much higher than 100 percent; the dealer will double, triple, or even quintuple his actual cost. Finding the correct price just takes a little research. If the dealer's asking $700 for the sun roof, call some sunroof installers and they'll give you the identical item for $295. Pinstripes $125? The guy at the corner auto body shop will put some on for you for $15.

Preparation Charges

The factory price on the car already includes a margin for dealer preparation. True, there's a kid working out back who will wash the car for you and scrape a big glob of glue off the bumper before you drive it home. But don't pay anything extra for "dealer prep." If you want to spend something for "dealer prep," walk back to the service area, find the kid who's cleaning your car, and tip him five bucks. He's probably the only person at the dealership who deserves the extra money.

Processing Fees

Processing fees are a scam to raise the price of every car by just a little extra. When you sign for the car, you'll be signing a sales agreement that lists the price of the car and the taxes that you pay on it. Just below the price of the car, there's often printed into the form a *totally bogus* processing fee, usually in bold numbers: $99.00 or $180.00 or whatever. It's printed on the form, very official looking.

Just cross it out. It's totally negotiable. If you don't cross it out, you'll notice that when the dealer fills out the finance agreement, the $99.00 "processing fee" will be added to the price of the car.

This scam works so well because of all the other times in life we pay processing fees: $21 to register your car, $25 for a marriage license. It's a clever way for the dealer to get a little extra once you've already agreed on the price of a car. Tell him, nicely, that you're not paying this $99.00 fraud fee and that you're willing to buy the car elsewhere. They won't pass up the deal for this piddling amount.

Extended Service Plans

This is a scam that all sorts of retailers push these days, for a reason: high profit at very little expense.

Just as TV salesmen try to sell you that extended

service contract when you buy a TV, the car dealer will try to push a little add-on to the warranty, at a price of many hundreds of dollars.

Repair bills can be scary. So why aren't extended service plans a good idea? First of all, these service contracts sometimes don't cover the kinds of repairs you are likely to need. The insurance that you buy is over-priced for what it does cover. Even more upsetting is the fact that such contracts are a tool to rob more money from you later on, since the warranty work will have to be done at the dealer's rip-off service department (more about that to follow). Dealers are experts at "finding" new problems with your car when it happens to be in their shop. If you ever do take your car in for some "extended warranty service," you will usually find that: (a) your problem is not really covered, and (b) "by the way, we've discovered these two other problems that we have fixed for only $377.58." Once again, the dealer sees the service contract as another opportunity for hundreds of dollars of pure profit.

Credit Life Insurance

This crock of garbage is usually sold to you by the finance guy. Credit life insurance, which pays off the car loan in case you die, is really overpriced for insurance and a thoroughly bad idea. Whether you've got a family or not, regular life insurance is a better way to pay debts should you die. If you have no family to protect, you may not want any insurance at all. Credit life insurance from a car dealer is expensive and represents hundreds of dollars of profit for the dealer and the finance man. If you want some insurance for your debts in case you die or are disabled, go out and buy some from a respectable insurance agent, who will give you much better coverage at much lower prices.

Accident, Health, and Disability Insurance

More bogus stuff from the finance guy. It is hard to find a worse deal on insurance! Car dealers are a case study in how to provide poor or neglible insurance cover-age at outrageous rates. Once again, there are hundreds of dollars of profit for the dealer, and beans for you. Your regular auto and health insurance should do fine: if you don't have any, by all means, get your car and your health insured, but don't buy insurance from a car dealer! Genuine, full-time respectable insurance agents have a reputation to preserve, but the car dealer who may never see you again could care less if you get cheated by high rates and inadequate coverage.

A Final Warning About the Finance Man

You can't overestimate the need to be cautious with the finance guy, or whoever's on duty to wrap up the deal. Sometimes he never even mentions the extras he wants to unload on you: he tries to sneak them by on the forms you sign. I've seen this scam over and over again. You're in the finance office, tired, bleary-eyed, sick of the whole thing, anxious to wrap up the deal and go home, and the finance guy has his computer spit out the final sales/financing agreement. When you look at the agreement, you find that your signature will say that you agreed to buy credit life insurance and all the other garbage listed under this heading, including the rust-proofing that you already told the salesman you don't want. You'll find that the finance guy's sneaky tricks have added more than $2,000 to the total purchase price. The finance guy is also, at many dealers, charged with the duty of switching the numbers on you. The $9,677.98 that you agreed on becomes $9,987.76, and 12.25 percent interest rate becomes 15.25 percent on the car loan. Death by firing squad is too good for this man.

Check that Final Agreement Carefully. In those final minutes, the finance man will pull out all the stops to cheat you. Don't sign until you're fully satisfied that the paperwork is entirely clean of all the options and extras you don't want.

6

Psychological Strategies of Car Salesmen

The real experts on human nature aren't psychologists, they're the guys who are making $100,000 a year as top car salesmen or sales managers. It is keen perception of human nature that makes a good salesman as effective as he is. Although car salesmen are well practiced at deceiving customers, you don't need much armor to resist them. They can only succeed at manipulating you if you are ignorant or uncertain about the car-buying process. If you're unsure of yourself, your uncertainty is an Achilles heel, a window of vulnerability, to the auto-sales staff. The salesman has practiced a hundred different lies that will help separate you and your money. However, if you know how the racket operates—if you know that they're working to deceive you—you become invincible.

The Shell Game

The shell game is about false discounts that are not really discounts.

A car dealer can potentially make $4,000 or more in profit from a single car purchase: on the price of the car itself, on the rustproofing, the interest rate, the extended service plan, and so on. This means that the dealer has $4,000 he can play with in a shell game while selling you a car. His basic trick is to give you a discount in one area and then rob you blind in another. Whenever a dealer has an alleged "sale" ($2,000 off! 6.6 percent financing!), he merely takes a portion of that $4,000 and offers it to you up front. The great giveaway is possible because the dealer will keep a high profit margin in another area. (Sure, you can get a $2,000 discount on a new car. But that is $2,000 off the price of the car as marked on the add-on sticker, with an additional dealer markup, or ADM, of $1,500 and required rustproofing priced at $995.) There are many varieties of the shell game, e.g., a guaranteed $1,000 for your trade-in. Once again, a portion of the original $4,000 profit potential is merely offset by a price increase in some other area.

The dealer's generosity in one area is a good tactic for the negotiations. "After all, we gave you $1,400 off the price of the car, it's only fair that you take rustproofing at full price. We've got to make a living, too." Whenever the dealer gives discounts with a smile, he is playing the shell game. He is hoping to keep your eyes on the shell with the discount, while he moves around the shells that hide the real money.

It is not hard to see why the shell game works. The dealer, like a good street magician, is working hard to distract you from what is really taking place. The scale of money involved is a big help here. *I got $1,000 off!* Pretty exciting stuff. It's not every day you save $1,000. That's why the car racket is so successful—the lies sound so good. So what if the dealer used his $1,000 discount as a lever to cheat you out of $3,000 more? What's important is that you're excited with the *thought* of getting a great deal. "A good deal," the dealers always say, "is in the mind of the customer." Yes, indeed.

When buying a car, you've got to get used to playing ball with the big boys. The big boys toss around $1,000 like a poker chip. Now that you've read this book, you'll find that buying a car is a confidence-building experience. Just wait until you feel that rush of power when you realize that you've saved several thousand dollars.

The shell game does more than distract you from big discounts by giving you one or two small ones. It is also meant to fool you into thinking that you've been lucky enough to get a special deal because of your good looks or timing or whatever.

It can be pretty exciting to get one of these shell—game discounts. "Just for you, sir, to thank you for buying a car on this rainy day, I'll give you and your lovely wife an all-expense-paid weekend of your choice in the honeymoon suite at the Hyatt, with a lovely Sunday brunch included. Now don't you want to sign right here?" Of course the car dealer has a special deal with the hotel, and the $250 for the honeymoon suite barely makes a dent in the dealer's $3,000 profit on the car deal.

The two most effective shell-game plays are the buydown to a low financing rate (2.5 percent! I can't believe it!) and the offering of too much money for a trade-in. Once a customer was hemming and hawing about a new $25,000 Corvette. His trade-in was worth about $4,500, and he knew it. The salesman hadn't convinced the customer to buy; he was hesitating and wanted to keep looking. All of a sudden the manager appeared—he had been slyly keeping an eye on things.

"Hey!" the manager shouted to his assistant. "Try and find whoever owns the blue Buick!"

"Why, that's me," said the Corvette shopper.

"You know," said the manager, "we got a customer in used cars this morning who was just dreaming of a classic blue Buick Regal like yours. He'd pay $7,500 for it, he said, way over what it's worth, and I'll give you $6,500 right now for it just to gamble I can get him back in here. I can't pay cash, but if you could find your way to trade that Buick for any car in the place, I'll give you a deal right now, on the spot—you'll never be able to find one like it again. Six and a half thousand, on the spot. We'll finance the rest."

"Sixty-five hundred for my old Buick? Really?" said the customer.

"Yeah, you're lucky I had that customer looking for it. An amazing coincidence, huh?" (Actually, no such customer existed.)

"Maybe I will take that Corvette," said the customer, heading back toward the lot to look at his new car.

"You see," said the manager to the salesman when the

customer was out of earshot. "You just gotta be a little creative with these people. Sure, we'll give him two grand extra for the Buick. But you can bet he's payin' full price for that 'Vette, and you still got a nice commission. Get out there and buy him a soda, will ya?"

Negotiating for a new car is like dealing with that ancient mythological many-headed monster, the Hydra. Every time you cut off one head of the nasty monster, one or two more spring up. Thus it is with a car dealer. Sure, he'll cheerfully give you a discount in one area, but he'll be cheating you in two other ways at the same time.

When the salesman plays the shell game, pretend that you've gotta shovel to bang on every head of the monster as soon as each one crops up. Bang on the dealer markup! The rustproofing! The credit life insurance! The too-low or too-high bid on your trade-in! Negotiating a car deal requires nothing more than insisting on *every* discount you are owed. It means not being fooled by the shell game. You want your car at full discount, with no monster heads popping out from under the hood. The $500 or so profit that the dealership will take in the very best of car deals is more than enough. Not to mention that they will still succeed in robbing many other customers of an extra $3,000 or so.

The Jigsaw Puzzle

The jigsaw puzzle is the dealer's way of creating such confusion that you won't know you're getting cheated, or will be too lost to deal with it.

Buying a car is complicated. So many times people say to me, "Leslie, how do I get a good deal on a car?" I tell them to read this book. It's just not the kind of thing you can describe in a couple of sentences.

The confusion starts the moment you start dealing. For example, if you have a trade-in, dealers often *won't* tell you the price of the new car, and *won't* tell you what they're giving you for a trade-in offer. Instead, they'll present you with a "difference" figure, that is, the difference between the price of the new car and the value of the trade-in. *"Ma'am, we can send you home in that brand-new, beautiful car for only $6,742 difference. Now that's not much, is it? Six grand for a nice new car like that?"*

Once, when I was doing my undercover routine, the manager sent me down to the customer with a "difference" offer and said: "Okay, Leslie, now go down there and confuse 'em good."

Even if the car business were honest, buying a car would be complicated: prices, options, extras, financing—that's enough of a hassle right there—plus the wide range of fraud tricks that car salesmen try to pull that you must consider.

But, like many things, car buying is not as complicated as it might seem. Car dealers would like to keep the car-buying process as complex and mysterious as possible because the complexity helps them make money. Lawyers make money because of the feeling on the part of the client that law is too complicated to understand by himself—so he trusts a lawyer to handle it for him. An attorney may be expensive, but at least he takes care of things. Car dealers hope to be "professionals" in the same way. *"You like the car? Good. We'll be happy to take care of things for you. Yes, sir, I agree, there is a lot of paperwork here. Just let me fill it out for you—I've got a lot of experience with this, after all—and I'll just show you where to put your autograph. Yes, sir, car sales have certainly changed since the old days. We have to be real professionals now in order to give the customer the service he deserves. Just sign here, and here, and here . . ."*

The public really does not like hassles, and people will gladly lose thousands of dollars rather than deal with something complicated. Income tax is the prime example. Filling out tax forms is such a pain in the neck that many of us lose thousands of dollars in legitimate deductions just because it's too complicated to get hold of the correct forms and fill them out. The car dealer hopes you will feel the same way about buying your car. You can save as much money buying a car as you do taking all the correct tax deductions, but I would rather argue with a car salesman than sit down with some tax forms any day.

The key to defeating the jigsaw puzzle, in a nutshell, is to make your purchase slowly, step-by-step, making sure you understand everything that is going on. Make sure that every item on every form you sign is justified. If necessary, go home and reread the relevant section of this book until you feel confident that you are doing the right thing.

The Endurance Game

Car buying can be such a hassle, you'll sign because you are too tired to argue.

This manipulative strategy is a close cousin of the jigsaw puzzle. Buying a car is often a lengthy process, much different from buying a box of chocolates over the counter. It's hard to leave a dealer with your new car in under three hours. We all hate hassles, and car dealers know this: they make our fear of hassles work to their advantage. To a point, they will make things as smooth and easy for you as possible. If you will buy the car at full price, they will even bring all the paperwork to your home or office for you to sign. But if you want to bargain, if you want to save yourself a few thousand, they will make the purchase quite difficult.

Our hatred of hassles is so strong that after several hours in a car showroom, the numbers can become unreal. You're hungry, you're thirsty, you want to get out of the stuffy showroom, away from the greasy salesmen. "So what's a few more hundred?" you ask yourself, "Let's get it over with!"

Sometimes a salesman will go to another room and have a couple of cigarettes in order to make you wait longer. He hopes that your frustration will make you give in more easily. One time I overheard the following conversation in the salesmen's rest room:

"Hey Rudy, got anything cookin'?"

"Naw, blew my last customer out the door. How about you?"

"Yeah, I got some guy out there, figures he's a sharp customer. Thought I'd make him stew awhile. I'm supposed to be reevaluating his trade right now. [Chuckles.] You wanna go out to McDonald's? We can go out the back in my new demo."

"Sure, but what about your customer?"

"We'll be back in about 20 minutes, he should be all stewed up by then. He'll be ready to sign." The moral is: bring a good book to read when you come to the showroom.

It's good to go shopping for a car with a full stomach. If you get hungry in the middle of your negotiations, take a break: your five-dollar lunch might save you 500. Take it slow. Relax, have a soda, take a walk around the showroom: conduct things at your own pace.

I've noticed, too, that buying a car is a lot more of a hassle when you don't know what you're doing. Your feeling of anxiety and confusion increases as the salesmen sell you this extra and that extra, and you argue about this and that but aren't really sure of your reasoning. Because you feel unsure and, quite correctly, in danger of being cheated, your natural impulse is to want to end the pain by closing the deal quickly.

Now that you're armed with correct information, you can treat car shopping as a game rather than a hassle. Since it's a game you will win, you shouldn't mind waiting a bit for them to lose. Your time at the car dealer will pass quickly as you carefully progress toward your goal. You're nearing that magic moment when the salesman gives in and shakes your hand. A great car and a great deal! You'll love it.

A little bit of sheer willpower is necessary during those two or three hours at the dealer, I admit. But it's more than worth it to save a few thousand, to enjoy that feeling of winning.

But I hate hassles, you say! I'm too successful and important to bother with any low-life car salesman! Buying a car is just something you have to do yourself—there isn't any way to do it in ten minutes.

The Intimidation Game

You are the customer. You are going to spend thousands of dollars on a major purchase, so have every right to expect the automobile sales staff to be polite, if not downright humble. But not so! Car salesmen have a lot of success—an awful lot of success—by intimidating their customers into buying cars.

The salesman will at times play the authority figure who commands obedience. Modern life is complicated—the days are long past when a wise adult could know just about everything there is to know. We rely on experts all the time—to tell us the weather, to fix our microwave oven, to book a good hotel—to help us through life's difficulties. Even though you think of yourself as an independent adult, you still, regrettably, have to spend a lot of time doing what you're told. The sign tells you to go one way, the nurse tells you to take off your clothes, the boss tells you to follow the company rules. In many ways you're used to getting ordered around, especially by "experts." It's different from the old days when Attila the Hun would stand, mighty and strong, and order brave men to go hither and yon. Today authority comes in the form of a guy in a white coat who tells you what procedure to follow, and you listen partly because you trust him and partly because you don't know what else to do. It is this quiet, modern, bureaucratic type of authority that a car dealer seeks to imitate; you are expected to obey because you are in the presence of "experts in the field."

Salesmen are taught never to say please or use other phrases that might imply a choice or otherwise give the customer a chance to say no. The idea is for the salesman to be friendly but authoritative at all times. Most of the time the natural politeness of people prevents them from refusing to go along or interrupting the salesman's commands and flow of questions. At one dealer the managers told us to lead the customers around the various buildings at the dealership until they were lost and therefore felt dependent on us.

One time a Chevy salesman bet another that he could make the next random customer who came in the door lie down flat in the backseat of a white Monte Carlo on the showroom floor. For five bucks he was on. A customer approached. "How are you today, sir?" the salesman began. He steered the customer over toward the Monte Carlo, at the same time talking about the new comfort of Chevy interiors. Opening the door and pulling forward the front seat of the Monte Carlo, the salesman said, "Now just sit right down there in the back, sir, and see what I mean." The man sat down. "Now lie down!" he barked. The customer's hands went up as his body went flat on his back. "Isn't that nice?" said the salesman, referring not only to backseat comfort but also to the ease of dominating customers and the joy of winning five dollars.

The authority of the car salesman needs just one element to make it fully effective: time. One of the odd truths about human nature is that the people you spend time with shape your frame of mind. After several hours at a car dealership, you're already influenced by the salesman, whether you like it or not. His natural authority as an expert in an unfamiliar setting is reinforced by his guidance over your activities, and his responsiveness to your questions and needs for the last several hours. After some time on the dealer's lot, you're probably more comfortable with the idea of buying a car than when you first came in. It can seem very, very natural to sign those papers and take a car home, all the while trusting the salesman to give you a great deal.

How do you fight the authority routine? Car salesmen's authority depends on your ignorance. You know now that they're not experts or professionals. For the most part, they're just a bunch of sleazy people making money off of folks who don't know better. Even if you looked at them as professionals—and some of them do know a lot about the cars they sell—remember that they will fib because it comes down to their own pocketbook. Just think of the practice of medicine: an honorable and learned field, to be sure, with every legitimate doctor a professional, but as many as one out of every five operations in the United States is unnecessary. Why? So doctors can make more money! Don't think car salesmen are any nobler.

Surprising as it may seem, car salesmen will bully you if he thinks it will work. You're about to spend all that money—you'd think they would be nice. But car salespeople are clever. They will try unexpected approaches in order to catch you off balance. One way is by bullying you, intimidating you, and making you feel small.

Car salesmen are often street tough as well as smart. Part of their act is to yell, bluff, and intimidate when it suits their purpose. The intimidation works because of the basic uncertainty of the car buyer. As you start to negotiate, the salesman might shout: "How *dare* you call me a liar! I'm working hard to give you a good deal, and you call me a liar!"

"Oh, well, gee, I'm sorry," the customer often replies.

Some of us make the mistake of taking someone's bullying at face value. If someone's bullying us, we think that the bully has either the right to do so or the power to get away with it. And yet neither of these is necessarily true. Car salesmen especially, scoundrels that they are, have no right to be impolite. But being clever, they know that bullying works on some people—it will just trigger an automatic reaction of obedience.

If you are unsure of your credit standing or your ability to finance the car, you are all the more vulnerable to intimidation. There's an interesting bit of reverse psychology about financing. Even though you still pay for the car and pay interest on the money you borrow, you may still feel as if the lenders are doing you a favor. If a friend lends you money, he is doing you a favor, of course. But when a bank or a finance company lends you money, it's strictly business—so there's no need to feel submissive.

Intimidation is only possible when you are unsure of yourself. Now that you know car salesmen are scoundrels, you'll know they have no right to intimidate you. They have no right to order you around. It's natural when someone yells at you to have a moment's hesitation: Who is this person? Does he really have power over me?

If ever a car salesman or manager barks at you, bark right back. He'll know you aren't someone to be messed with. Even if you have shaky credit and you'd like to apply for dealer financing, it is still good to insist on politeness. Your confidence will actually help you get the loan approved!

The salesman will also try to make you feel guilty about not doing what he wants.

"After all the time I've spent showing you new cars, you're going to pick up now and buy a car from someone else? Is that the way you appreciate my time and effort? Is that how you treat your friends?"

"I'm new here as a salesman, and my boss is gonna fire me unless I sell a car this week. Please, I'm giving you a great deal here. You wouldn't want me to lose my job."

"How can you even say I'm not telling the truth? I wouldn't have taken this job unless it was honest. You know you're really hurting my feelings."

I've really heard these hokey lines from car salesmen, and they work. But guilt is an entirely inappropriate reason for buying a car. Just because the salesman bought you a Coca-Cola and a giant Snickers bar, you don't have to buy a $12,000 car from him. The salesman makes his living talking to customers. Some buy a car and some don't. So there's no need to feel guilty if a salesman spends a lot of time with you and you leave him empty-handed.

There is no reason to buy the wrong car, or the right car at the wrong price, just because a salesman has spent time with you. Do you buy stuff from every salesperson, every store clerk who talks with you? Of course not. It's part of doing business. A car salesman may spend four hours with you and you won't buy anything. Sure. But tomorrow he may make $1,000 in his first two hours at work. He knows that, it's the nature of the job.

There's no reason to feel guilty about bargaining hard with a salesman, either. At worse, he's going to make about $150 from your purchase of the car. That's not bad for a few hours' work. Most Americans don't make that much money even after a long, hard day. So when he says, "Hey, I've got to make a living, too," don't think he's near starvation.

The Trust-Me Game

It's a very evil world, yet most of us keep hoping that we will not be disappointed by our trust in others. Every good car salesman works very hard to convince you that, at least this once, you have met an honest car salesman. He will work hard to influence you by creating a false feeling of friendship.

Recently a noted evangelist declared that loneliness may be America's number-one problem. Sometimes I think he is right. Nothing produces happiness like the gift of human companionship, and nothing makes life more miserable than a lack of human warmth. So much of modern society produces loneliness: the separation of families, the devotion to careers, the mobility and transitory nature of modern living. We all need friends, whether we admit it or not. Some of us don't have enough friends, or at least enough good ones.

Buying a car is exciting because you get the undivided attention of a human being for a significant span of time. Attention is a wonderful thing. Just think, when you go shopping for a car, a $60,000-a-year "marketing specialist" is willing to spend an entire afternoon with you while you fuss over colors and engine configurations. When you are negotiating, there are high-level meetings about you. When I was buying my last car, I had a peek into the room where the sales staff was meeting. Even though I know that they were merely plotting to trick this strange customer into paying a higher price, I was flattered: three superb sales minds, earning a quarter of a million dollars a year among them, were meeting to discuss *me*. Gosh, it was exciting!

On auto-shopping day, it really can seem as if you have made a new friend. Some of these guys are so good at it! Many of these salesmen, however, will only be friendly to you in the future if you bring them another customer. And their proffered friendship will not prevent them from their main goal of taking your money.

I recall a night when I was helping a friend to buy a car. We got to the dealer around 8:00 P.M., and the negotiations were complete by midnight. (A dealer never closes on a paying customer. The staff stays until you take your new car home rather than risk losing you to another dealer.) I was standing out on the lot next to my friend's new car, which we were ready to take home. The salesman, the manager, the finance guy all emerged in turn. I said hello and we talked about cars and nightlife and women—it was a genuinely warm moment. Yet these same people had all been lying to us and trying to take my friend's money for the last several hours. But the battle was over, and we were now just people—like that classic Warner Brothers cartoon in which the sheepdog and the coyote, after a hard day's battle, punch the time clock and go home the best of friends.

The ability to charm, to convey human warmth, to use your good human qualities to induce a vulnerable trust in your customers: these are the skills of a top car salesman. I was told I would be great at it. One manager told me: *"You've got such a sincere face. When you look someone right in the eye with those blue eyes of yours—especially the women, they will love you—you'll have them eating out of your hand and signing those papers right and left. You're gonna be a star. $80,000 a year at least."* I hope I do convey that sense of trustworthiness. But I am an honest man, not a poseur, and that's why I couldn't stay in the car business.

Many people are shocked when I point out how they've been robbed at a car dealer. "But the salesman seemed so nice! How could he be such a thief and be so friendly!" Yes, indeed. How could he?

It's a mistake to think that being greedy and wicked prevents you from being nice and friendly. After all, many dictators were known as nice guys to their close friends. And all of us, nice as we are, are capable of little fibs when it suits us. I agree, you have to be a pretty thick-skinned rat to be a lying car salesman for any length of time. The stress takes a very high toll on some of them. But in a society that worships money as much as ours does, many of these salesmen find it is worth the effort to pretend friendliness while stealing someone's wallet.

There is very little in the world that is as seductive as human warmth. We will do a lot for our friends, and sometimes we will do things we shouldn't. It is important to remember that a car salesman is not your friend, and cannot be, because his job is to take your money. Very sadly, the car salesman often makes his biggest profits from people who are the most vulnerable, people who need friends, people who want to trust, people who don't want to let a new friend down.

The power of human warmth is a curious phenomenon. Even people who know, in theory, that auto sales is a crooked business will often come home saying, "Yeah, but I met this salesman who was *really nice;* he was obviously different, and I felt really comfortable buying a car from him." Salespeople work hard to create that impression. Another favorite trick is to blame all the bad-guy stuff on the manager. The managers don't mind, of course, because it helps profits. With this scheme, the salesman will tell you, *"Sure, there's a discount, I don't know what the manager will go for, but I'll do my best for you. You know, I'm really out to sell a car here, and I'll work hard to give you the best deal possible! You're obviously good people, and I'd like to do something for you. You folks are really nice, the kind of people I like to see happy with a new car."*

This is why it's good to go car shopping with a real friend, so that you don't get taken in by the friendliness of the friendly salesman.

The salesman will try to relax you with his smoothness. *"Let me tell you, ma'am, I've helped a lot of intelligent young ladies like yourself buy cars. Every one of them has gotten a great deal and has gone home with a good, trouble-free car. In fact, there's a few that call me every now and then just to say hello and tell me how the new car is running. If you should have any service problems at all, ma'am—not that you will, with this fine car—just give me a call and I'll have it taken care of right away!"*

After all, look at the salesman's card: Leslie R. Sachs, Automotive Sales Specialist. "My, that's impressive! I bet he knows what he's doing." One manager at "Car School" even suggested that we cultivate authority in the style of a physician. "After all," he said, "some of you guys make as much money as a doctor. Remember, the customer is as lost in the dealership as he is in a doctor's office. Well, you show him what to do. So when it comes time to tell him to sign, he signs."

It might sound silly, but it works. First of all, it is true that you can get lost in a modern auto-dealership, with its maze of offices, departments, front lots, back lots, and side lots. Even some of the salesmen can't find all the new cars in stock. A psychological factor leads to confusion, too. You mean people actually exchange thousands of dollars each day, right here? I've always been so puzzled by financing. How does it work? I know you're supposed to negotiate. I wonder if I can get a good deal—whatever that is?

Moreover, human beings faced with an unfamiliar environment tend to look for someone to trust. You need a friend. Who becomes your friend? Of course, the friendly salesman, who gently takes you under his wing as he becomes your guide through car land. In times of uncertainty you will obey someone who seems to be both friendly and knowledgeable.

After you've finished this book, however, and after you've shopped for one or two cars, you will be the expert, the one who knows the score on the auto business. And you'll know that these car people are not to be trusted, not as far as you can throw them.

The Ego Game

Our self-image is important to us. We care about the image we project to other people, even if they are strangers. Car salesmen are experts at taking advantage of your desire to project a good image. They know that you will sometimes pay thousands of extra dollars just to protect your ego—so it's important to know how salesmen play the ego game.

Understanding the auto racket can lead to a big ego boost after you triumph in the showroom battle of wits. Saving money and not letting salesmen take advantage of you makes you more confident and self-assured.

You might say, "Aw, I don't care what any lousy car salesman thinks of me. I'm in no danger of the ego game." But even if you look down your nose at car salesmen, they can twist the ego game so that you seem to be harming your own image of yourself by not doing what they want. All of us like to see ourselves in certain ways, and car salesmen like to arrange it so that you spend more money to protect your self-image. It is simply human nature to care what other people think. You care about what the people around you are thinking, and after several hours in a car dealer, that bunch of stooges does begin to matter to you somehow. Here's how they play the ego game.

First of all, there is your desire not to contradict yourself. Our society and our culture fetishize people who know what they are doing, people who are decisive and know what they want. I say, marshmallows! You don't learn things unless you experiment. Also, when you are making a really big decision, you have a perfect right to consider different options and change your mind. Salesmen like to praise you for being "decisive," which, in their minds, means easy to manipulate and quick to give in.

Both men and women are afraid of changing their minds and appearing too flighty. "So, what do you *want*, then?" whines the salesman, suggesting that you are less than stable for considering more than one alternative. Take your own sweet time. You've got all day, and so does the salesman—who will make more than a day's pay from your purchase. At a car dealer, you will find yourself learning things about cars and about what you want in a car. Halfway through the negotiation, you may realize that you really want a smaller car. Or you may find that you really want the white one. Or you may feel, when the paperwork is in front of you, that even though you can afford the payments, you would be just as happy with a less expensive car. You *must not be shy* about telling them what you want, of telling them that you have changed your mind. Oh, of course they'll be annoyed— and they'll try to make you feel bad about it. *"So, you're not sure of what you want, are you? But you said you liked the gray sedan! What's the matter with you? Don't you mean what you say? You liked the car, didn't you? You drove the car, it was nice, wasn't it? You said then you wanted to buy it, didn't you? Well?"*

Your desire not to contradict yourself is a powerful lever to get you to buy the car in the first place. While you're being shown a car, the salesman will often ask a question like, "If we could make this car affordable for you, would you like to take it home?" if you give anything resembling an affirmative response, the salesman will later say, "You said you wanted to take this car home, didn't you?" Lots of people will go along, half nervous about their decision but reluctant to admit that they were too hasty.

This self-contradiction technique is used over and over again in the sales routine. "It's good for a car to be guarded against rust, isn't it?" Oh, sure, you say. "What do you mean you don't want rustproofing—you said yourself a car was better off with rust protection, didn't you?"

Salesmen are never ashamed of contradicting themselves, and indeed, they do it over and over again. "I'm sorry, there's no discount on the new models." Half an hour later, when you are arguing on a figure $700 below the sticker price, remember what the salesman said earlier! In every car negotiation, you wind up getting a price that the salesman at first said was impossible. So, if the salesman doesn't mind changing his tune again and again, you should feel no qualms about changing your own mind about what you want to do.

Particularly if you are not sure about what is going on, if you feel lost, say halt, go home, and read my book again. Don't feel guilty. It is your right. The salespeople will be glad to see you when you come back. You will get the same discount again, too, even though they will start with the lie that, "I'm sorry, the special price we were

able to offer you yesterday was only good for that day."
Yeah, sure.

Another vulnerability is your need to pretend you understand what's going on. We all hate to feel stupid. Sometimes we will even spend money just to avoid looking stupid. And yet you only look smart to a car salesman when you don't waste your money.

"Every intelligent person gets rustproofing on their car," said one salesman, while another one stood by and nodded gravely. "Of course," said the customer, not wanting to look dumb and get left off the bandwagon. Don't fall for this kind of stuff. It's much better to ask questions and, as I said above, say no to *everything* extra they try to sell you. Especially when in doubt, say no. Ask the salesman for reasons. Remember, you can't trust a single thing he says. Of course he will tell you that "Everybody does this, everybody knows this, we're a reputable dealer!"

The ego game is a powerful one, and once again, its basic prerequisite is your uncertainty. I think one of the most powerful human motivations is the fear of being embarrassed. Thus dealers tell you, "Of course, anyone would see that you're being offered the deal of a lifetime here." Even if you guess that they might be cheating you royally, a little voice inside of you says, "But these guys might be honest, and this might be a great deal. In which case I'll really be a fool if I try to question them. They'll know I'm an idiot. Oh well, it's probably not too bad of a deal. I guess I'll just go along with it." In truth, you have no reason to be ashamed of asking questions, saying no, or postponing your decision.

It is human nature to deny that you are being cheated, even when you know you are.

People often ask me: "Leslie, if the car business is so crooked, how come so few people know about it? Why do all these dealers have great reputations?" One of the paradoxes of the whole business is that, though dealers succeed in deceiving and robbing people on a massive scale, most of the victims are eager to deny it. Being victimized by a car dealer is somewhat humiliating: after all, you personally lost out where others have won. So the tendency is to convince yourself that, "Well, I guess I got a pretty good deal."

Salesmen do what they can to reinforce this. "You got a great deal, miss. You should be mighty happy." Once a manager told me, "I sold a car to this one guy, really took the shirt off his back. Then, in the lot, as he was taking the car away, he said to me, 'Listen, be honest with me. Just let me know, did I really get a good deal?' And I said, 'That's right, you really did get a good deal.' And you know, he went home happy. A good deal, you know, is always in the mind of the customer."

When you feel helpless about being cheated, you want to deny what happened. You want to pretend that things went your way. If the salesman has done everything to convey a friendly, helpful image while he takes your money, you will be all the more likely to pretend things are great. You may even write a letter to the friendly rip-off artists to tell them what nice guys they are.

Perhaps this happened to you the last time you bought a car. You were in the middle of negotiating the deal, but you got the sick feeling that you were being cheated. You weren't absolutely sure, though, and so you were reluctant to stop things. Or you knew you were getting cheated, but just didn't know what to do about it. Your natural tendency is not to think about it, to pretend that nothing bad happened, to lie to yourself by saying, "Well, I handled things about as well as I could." Inside of your mind a bell might have rung. You remembered the friend who recommended that you read Dr. Sachs's book before you went car shopping. Oh well, you say, too late for that.

Another motive is the fear of not going along with the gang.

Every once in a while car dealers have "sale events." You know, clowns on the car lot (the kind with big round noses, not just the usual salesmen), candy for the kids, balloons everywhere. Car dealers have discovered that people love to be cheated in groups.

It's funny that car dealers don't take more trouble to hide the negotiating process from other customers. Often the little booths are right off the showroom floor, and if you stand there quietly, you can hear the salesmen repeating the standard lies in one booth after another. "Let me give it to you straight, miss . . ." If you're a crook, it pays to be open about it, to act like there's nothing wrong. And hey, everybody's doing it, everybody's signing those papers, with full rustproofing and the works!

Most all of us love the idea of being on a team. We don't like to let the team down, even if the team is a bunch of scoundrels. After all, you've gotta support your team, don't you? After a few hours with a car dealer, you're a part of the team. You're a big part of the day for everyone at the dealership. The managers are thinking hard about your personality; your name is written on a bulletin board somewhere, waiting for check marks that record what you decide to do. But if you're a hard bargainer, you're definitely bucking the team mentality.

No, buying a car is not a team adventure. It's more like a Clint Eastwood spaghetti western—you against the whole crooked town. But don't worry, you've got a friend here in me and my book.

7

The Right Approach for Saving Thousands of Dollars

In this chapter I'll cover attitude and negotiating approach for getting a good deal on the car that you want. In the next chapter I'll cover the actual numbers, and show you how to compute and specify the right discount—the perfect deal—on the car that you select.

It should be great fun. You're confidently and successfully playing a big-league financial game. You'll probably be winning a battle with a millionaire (chances are the owner of the dealership *is* a millionaire). It's like dealing in oil wells with J. R. Ewing. Except that you know you're going to win because you won't deal until the price is right.

Once you start understanding how to play this game, you may find it to be as invigorating as tennis. "Hey, wanna go over to a car dealer and knock some heads today?" Seriously, though, there are few social games that provide the satisfaction of buying a car, once you know how to play to win. You triumph over the wicked and save yourself thousands of dollars all in one stroke. You're a social crusader and wheeler-dealer, all in one afternoon. That's hard to beat!

Your Power to Say No

You must feel free to say no in order to resist the lies and the pressure. It is an immense tool in your hands. A lot of us are out of the habit of saying no. We surround ourselves with nice people we have no need to refuse or deny. Or perhaps we are just too accommodating to our friends, our families, and our employers. But with a car dealer, you must recover your childlike joy in saying: no! You're the customer, you've got the money, and the power is in your hands. You say no until the deal is just right, until everything is to your satisfaction. You will find that your boldness in saying no will win you the grudging respect of the salesmen and the dealer.

Never Make Decisions Based on What a Salesman Says

By now you've been told enough of the vast range of a car salesman's lies to have an idea of how inventive and persistent they are in deceiving you. I hope I have conveyed how good the salesmen are at faking trust, honesty, and sincerity. (Remember, $70,000 a year is plenty of incentive.)

If you ever feel yourself trying to decide between two possible truths in a car dealership, never base your choice on what the salesman says. Note the direct connection between the salesman's lies and the money that he's trying to take from you. If you need more information, find out from someone else before you sign. Go back and read the relevant section of this book and, if necessary, compare at other dealers. But never trust the salesman, not a single word out of his mouth, unless that information isn't relevant to your purchase, e.g., "What's a good place to get a drink near here?"

If you mention having read this book (I'll tell you below why you shouldn't mention it), the saleman will try a number of ways to discredit the information you have. *"Aw, that guy did his research in 1979. Things have changed since then." "He lives near Washington, D.C. Everyone there is crooked." "It's all exaggeration. He was just trying to sell some books."* Don't you swallow it. You hold out for that good deal.

Don't Humiliate Salespeople—
Even If They Deserve It

Now that you've been reading this book on how to get a good car deal, you might feel tempted to walk into a dealer, slap this book on the table, and say, "Look. I know the whole crooked game you're playing. So don't try and mess with me! Give me the straight deal, the bottom-line price right now, or I'm leaving!"

It doesn't work that way. Although dealers do want to sell you a car, and will sell it to you at a good price, you have to remember that they're human beings, too. In order for you to get a good deal, you have to understand a bit of their psychology.

It is crucial to realize that car dealers must try to cheat you. On the theory that it never hurts to try—you never know what lies a customer will believe—the sales staff is devoted to doing their best to hoodwink you, regardless of how knowledgeable you seem to be about the sales racket. Besides, the salesmen are punished by the managers if they don't try. "Look, boss," a salesman might say, "this customer seems to know what she's doing."

"Baloney!" the manager will answer. "You go down there, charm her, and get a good profit on that car!"

It is a question of pride with the salesmen. They may be cold and calculating, but they are not robots. Every experienced car salesman is proud of his ability to hoodwink the customer, and so it becomes a matter of pride to take advantage of you. If you walk into the door demanding that the salesmen be honest for a change, you make it difficult for them to sell you a car. When I first started negotiating car deals, I used to make this mistake. If you bruise a salesman's or manager's ego too badly, he may *refuse* to sell you the car, even at a reasonable profit, just to protect that ego. I remember a time I spoke to a crooked saleswoman as follows: "Doesn't your conscience bother you?" I said. "You take advantage of people often, don't you? Especially if they're innocent and vulnerable, if they don't know any better.

You take every last dime you can, isn't that right?" She started crying and closed her folder. She told me to buy the car somewhere else. Oh sure, I had made a point. But the real point was to buy a car. So it's better if you play dumb.

I realize this is not easy. After all, when confronted with a group of irresponsible jerks, your first impulse is to put them in their place. But that is an entirely different goal from buying a car. If you put them down, they will get revenge on you the only way they have left—not selling you the car. And they will withhold the car even though the price is reasonable, just because it becomes a matter of pride. After all, they have lots of customers from whom they make thousands, and to them it can be worth the loss of a few hundred dollars just to get you upset. Once you're driving the car away, you can feel free to call them names.

I'm certainly not suggesting that you have an obligation to be nice to people who tell you dozens of lies and try to cheat you out of several thousand dollars. Anything you say to them will be mild compared to what they deserve. But it is important to have clearly in mind what you want to accomplish. Do I want to yell at a gang of cutthroats, or do I want to take a car home at a good price? It's your decision.

Beware of Your Desire to Have Your Toy Right Away

One of the most genuinely seductive aspects of the sales process is the car itself. It's beautiful; it drives well; you want it. I know that feeling. The salesman can tell that you want that car. His resolve is not to give it to you until you agree to his price and not yours.

It's funny how powerful that feeling is. A car is such a fantastic thing, such a wonderful gleaming hunk of metal and glass and motorized passion. You look at it and see all the fun you're going to have with it, how your neighbors and friends will be impressed, how much more wonderful your life will be. What is more, you want it now. Today. Right now. You're a big girl or boy. You're not little and don't have to wait for someone else to give you candy money. You want it, and you're big enough to buy it. They'll tease you by suggesting you can't afford it. "Whaddaya mean I can't afford it? I'll show you! Let me write that check! I can buy what I want, and I'll buy it now!"

At the dealership, the car you see, smell, and touch is much more real to you than the money you spend on it, which is no more than a figure in your checkbook. By temporarily refusing the discount you've requested, the salesman is threatening you, coming between you and the enjoyment of your toy. You know you could have the toy more quickly if you just agree with him and sign. And you are afraid you will not be able to take your toy home at all if you resist too long. "I'm sorry," the salesperson says. "We just can't do it at your price. It's our final offer." What if no one else has just this car, with the baby-blue pinstripe? You'll spend the next year grieving! Oh, what the heck, what's a few hundred, anyway? You sign.

I love cars—that's how I got into this in the first place—and even with everything I know about the crookedness of car dealers, from both sides of the negotiating table, even I feel the pull of a car I like. I'm tempted to say, oh, why not, give them a couple of extra hundred just to wrap it up and take my toy home. A top sales manager told me the same thing. "Buying a car," he said, "is an emotional rather than a rational experience. I'm no different. Here I am, auto-sales manager, making more than a hundred grand a year. And I see this classic Mercedes convertible I've always dreamed of. Did I get a good deal? No, not really, because I wanted my toy. I fell in love with the car; I would've paid even more for it than I did."

Salesmen are experts at playing the waiting game. They know when you're on the verge of giving in. You've just got to be resolved to hold firm, or else accept the loss of several hundred dollars or more—and the salesmen's laughter at you behind your back.

You can probably find the same car somewhere else, especially if there is a large city near you. With modern production automobiles, there are no one-of-a-kind items. If the price isn't right, you will probably find the identical car or an even better one somewhere else. Don't be surprised, too, if the same dealer calls you the next day with an offer to work things out to your satisfaction.

Shop with a Friend for Added Support

If you have a trusted friend who can go with you through the car-shopping process, by all means bring him along. Remember, though, it's a lot to ask of someone. He must be willing to sit with you through several hours of lot prowling, lies, and possible waiting. He may find it fun and educational as well, but it's definitely more than a quick jaunt.

Give your friend a brief survey of what you've learned about the crooked world of new car sales. Having a friend along makes you less vulnerable to the salesman's tricks. The salespeople may be conspiring against you, but you will have someone in your own little conspiracy to help you get a good deal. Having a friend makes your waiting time at the dealer more bearable. You can tell jokes about your car salesman while he consults with his manager, and you can talk about what a great car you're buying while you wait for your turn with the finance guy.

It's important, too, that your friend not force his or her own opinions on you. Your friend should not interfere with your getting the kind of car *you* like, even if that would not be her or his own choice.

Pretend to Be Uninformed and Visiting Your First Car Dealer

Even a crooked salesman only has so much energy. It is much easier on the salesman if he thinks of you as a customer he can easily deceive. He'll talk with you more openly, be under less stress, and his lies will be bigger (and thus more transparent). Salesmen, no less than customers, often blow a deal because they get sick of arguing. The salesman goes home without a sale, and you go home without a car. You should insist on a good price, but you must make it easy for the salesman to give that price to you. It all goes more smoothly if you act friendly and dumb.

The salesman's resistance is increased if he thinks of you as a know-it-all. He may spend a lot more time and effort trying to cheat you. Or he and the manager may quickly reach such a peak of frustration that they won't sell you the car, rather than admit defeat. It is likewise more difficult if they know you've been to other car dealers. They will want to know why you didn't buy a car somewhere else. The real danger of admitting you were at other dealers is that the salesman will think of you as hard to sell, and might give up trying to make the sale because of a fear that you won't buy from him either.

You get a good deal much more swiftly and surely by relaxing the salesman, by making him feel as if he is going to have an easy ride with you. When he presents the paperwork and you quietly ask for your whopping discount, you will have the element of surprise. Although he will be miffed by your stubborn insistence on your discount, he'll be less upset if he's thought of you as an uninformed car buyer all along.

In short, then, act ignorant about the whole process until it comes time to sign papers. Then hang on quietly to your request for a discount until you get it. You'll have a good chuckle at the look of astonishment on the salesman's face as you quietly demand $2,000 off the price he thought you would pay.

Another tactic: pretend that the discount you request is simply a matter of not wanting to spend more on a car. "Gee, I really like that car, but I just don't want to spend more than $8,700 on it. No, not another penny more. I'm very serious about keeping a high bank balance."

I go into dealerships and introduce myself as Dr. Sachs, which immediately tells the salespeople two things: (a)

I've got money, and (b) I'm a fuzzy-headed intellectual who knows nothing about car dealing. When I'm helping a woman buy a car, the salesman often assumes I am her lover, and that everything will be all smiles and high profits.

I don't tolerate rudeness, but otherwise I'm thoroughly polite and friendly. As we negotiate the price, I (or my friend) will act as if we just have some crazy idea of what is a good discount and no, we're sorry, but we're just not comfortable buying the car unless we get what we think is a good price. The management thinks of us as friendly idiots who just got lucky in guessing the numbers. And so before too long, we drive the car away. As I drive away on days like that, I've noticed two or three salesmen usually gather and look at me and my friend. "Gosh," they think, "that guy was different!" And they'll have the same respect for you, too.

Pretend to Be a Serious Shopper Ready to Buy Today

When you're buying a car, you will really have to work before the salespeople drop the veil of obscurity and lies. In order for them to do so, they have to believe you're a serious customer. You can't just go "shopping for prices," popping into a dealer or two to see what kind of discounts are available. That would be ridiculous anyway since almost all car dealers are the same. They will all give about the same discount to the sharp customer.

If you don't seem like a serious shopper, the salesman will spend most of his initial energy trying to determine if you are a buyer or a window shopper. He'll ask a question like, "How soon are you ready to buy a car?" It's best to put him at easy by saying, "Oh, I'm ready to buy today if I find the right car!" You'll hear him smack his lips. Now you can be sure of his undivided attention and his best efforts to give a good discount once the negotiations begin.

Even if you don't think you're going to buy from that

dealer—because you're unsure about the car or about the discount that you can get—it's still best to use the line about being ready to buy today. It's the only way to ensure that you'll get the attention that you need. And if you are fishing for price discounts as well as shopping for cars, it's the *only* way to press for a good discount.

You can always say no at the last minute, no matter how far the negotiations have gone, even if you've signed some papers—just so long as you haven't taken the new car home. (I'll say more about this below.)

When pretending to be a serious shopper, you must convey a perfect confidence that you can afford the car. Salesmen are trained to "qualify" the customer, i.e., check you out to see if you can afford the wheels you are looking at. He can waste a lot of time on this sort of talk. ("So, what do you do for a living?") Just act like money is no problem. Even if money is a problem, your confidence will help you arrange credit through the dealership. So walk up to a $14,000 car and say, "Hey! this is cheap!" Or ask, "would it be all right if I put $5,000 down? Could I finance the rest?" The salesman will get the message.

Make the Salesman and His Ego Work for You

It is a common human failing to play ego games. Now that you have become informed about the auto-sales racket, you might be tempted to play a few games of your own with car salesmen. "All right, you jerks, don't give me any guff."

But it is important to remember something often taught in business seminars: the most successful negotiations are usually carried out on a win/win basis. You get what you want when you find a way for somebody else to win, too. It's the same with a car: you win the car at the right price when you let the salesman feel he has had something of a victory.

Remember that the salesman, above all, wants to make a sale. He will be making decent money, even on a minimum-profit deal. Furthermore, the sale of your car will increase his total cars sold for the month and perhaps qualify him for a bonus. Unless you've tried to put him down (in which case he would send you home carless rather than admit that you got the better of him), he will make that deal.

The manager is putting pressure on the salesman, fueling him with lies, encouraging him to "keep a high gloss"—hold a large profit margin—on the car you're buying. As you become more insistent about your discount, however, the salesman will give up on his dreams of high profit and will become anxious to make a sale at all. The manager may come down and try to change your mind with his well-worn lies, but he, too, will ultimately settle for just making the sale if he can't hold a high profit.

Your overall attitude should be that you are doing them a favor by buying a car, for that in fact is the truth. I don't mean, "You jerks should be grateful I'm shopping here at all!" Rather, "I'd really like to give you guys my business. It would be so nice to buy a car from you, and I'll certainly do it if the price is right." Your friendliness and patience will show them that you care enough to give them a chance.

As the deal goes down to the wire—they're holding at $8438, while your freeze price is $8300—you should begin to massage his ego if the salesman is at all civil. "I really appreciate your spending all this time with me. I certainly hope your manager can agree to the price—I know you're doing your best." You can actually charm the salesman into giving you the benefit of the doubt. He'll tell the manager, "Come on, boss, these are nice people. What the heck, let's give 'em the car."

You should make him feel as if he's a good salesman. When the manager comes to talk to you, compliment him on his nice salesman and nice dealership, and thank him for spending time with you personally. This sort of talk can work like magic. As I keep saying, car salesmen are people, too. They spend their whole day cheating people who are principally concerned with themselves and their own wants. By treating the sales staff like human beings, you give them a kind of warmth they rarely see and don't deserve, but which they may appreciate enough to wrap up the deal for you. One manager even lamented at a sales meeting, "Some of these customers even work their charm on us," as if that were a scandalous and shocking thing.

In times of complexity and difficulty, a little courtesy never hurts.

Another, more specific way to do a salesman a favor has to do with the time of year you shop for a car. It's not really the case that there's a better time to shop: a sharp negotiator can get a good deal anytime and anywhere. But there are obviously certain times when the salesman and the dealer are more desperate to sell a car. Although you might not get a better deal, you might get a good deal more easily.

People love to buy a car on sunny Saturdays. Sometimes, in fact, Saturdays at the car dealer can be so busy that there aren't enough salesmen around, and they aren't anxious to spend a lot of time with a minimum-profit customer like yourself. Weekdays are better. Even better still are workday mornings or afternoons, when you might be the only customer in a dealership. Near the end of the month is also a good time, when salesmen are anxious to earn their bonuses and dealers are eager to fill their sales quotas. But best of all is a rainy day, when no one goes looking for cars. The salesmen are there, and they will sell you a car at a good price. They will feel lucky to have sold anything at all on such a day. You might go when it's raining (or snowing) just to enjoy the look of astonishment on the salesmen's faces as you walk onto the lot.

Don't Tell Them You've Read This Book

As I've said, this kind of thing may intimidate the salespeople. And they'll work double-time telling you lies about why the car business isn't as I describe it. You should just quietly enjoy your superior knowledge.

Once, after a long negotiating session, my friend was waiting for her car's final washing up and I was sitting with a group of salesmen when one of them asked me, "So, what do you do, Dr. Sachs?"

"I'm a writer," I said.

"What kind of things do you write?"

"I'm doing this book on how to get a good deal on a car."

They all laughed.

Now you can laugh, too.

Walk Out the Door Slowly

As I've said, car salesmen are not robots. Negotiating a car is more than a matter of plugging in the right formula: "Okay, I've read Dr. Sachs's book, and I know that the minimum-profit deal for you is about $10,200. Take it or leave it." That's not the way it works. A successful car negotiation takes time. There's a certain rhythm, a certain pace to it. The salesman must give himself a real shot at cheating you, or else he (and his manager) can't rest easy. You've just got to be patient while they fire their puffballs.

Remember, too, that's it's painful, psychologically speaking, for them to come down in price. The negotiating process will take some patience. The salesman is restrained by the manager from giving in too quickly. You must restrain yourself from giving in as well, or have a good friend around to hold you back.

Most important of all, remember that salesmen will work terribly hard to convince you that the discount you want is impossible. If they come down in price once, twice, or three times, they will try to convince you that any further discount is impossible, simply and absolutely impossible. You must be patient enough to wait this out.

Car salespeople are good at bluffing. They will say things like, "I'm sorry, that's the lowest we can go. If you can't take the car at that price, we'll just give you the deposit back and you'll have to leave the car for somebody else to buy." The salesman will look quite sincere, his folder of paperwork before him, seemingly quite ready to shake hands and say good-bye. You want that car, you're tempted to give in—but you shouldn't. You've got to outwait him. Say no again. "I'd really like you to ask the manager to approve the deal at the price I've already requested."

"I'm sorry," he might repeat. "It just can't be done."

"Well," you reply, "we'll just have to say good day." Get up very slowly, collect your things, and walk very slowly out the door. Pause to look at a few of the cars in the showroom, and maybe at a few more on the lot in front of the store window. The salesman will then have time to chase after you and say, "Wait just a minute!" Or even better, he will say with outstretched hand, "You've got a deal."

It's a sort of ballet, a dance of courtship, except what's being courted is your money and not you. Sometimes you want people to fuss over you before you believe they care. Likewise, car salesmen have to hassle you before they believe you can't be duped. You've simply got to wait them out. It takes them time to figure out that you are a sharp customer.

Negotiating a good deal is more involved than sitting down at a table and arguing. You only have enough pressure on them if you are really and truly ready to *walk away* from a bad deal. If you're at the table and are resolved to drive that car home tonight, the salesman will pick up the scent and will refuse to lower the price because he knows you want the car badly enough to give in to his terms. But if you have enough self-control to walk away, and are willing to prove it, you will probably get both the car and the good deal. Salesmen are very cautious about watching your sincerity as you threaten to leave. Many of them will actually wait until you've left the showroom and are walking toward your old car before they will run after you. It is a mind game, and the paradoxical truth is that he or she who is willing to lose the car will get both the car and the good deal.

8

The Terms of a Good Deal

Now we'll begin with the real financial essentials: what the dealer pays for the car and how much you should pay. Like everything else in car sales, the industry has conspired to make the truth both confusing and difficult to discover. A little care in reading this information will pay off in a big way in the salesman's office.

How much should you pay for a new car? If you just want a quick, rough formula, without any complicated explanations, here it is:

Take the factory sticker (see below)
Subtract 15% (or 12% on small, under $9,000 cars)
Add $600

This formula will, in many cases, be pretty close to the dealer's minimum profit of about $500. This formula is for a brand-new, typical American car. For certain hot items (don't trust the dealer as to what's hot), and many import cars, this formula will give you a number that's lower than the actual minimum sale price. But the formula will at least give you an idea of the scale on which the dealer is making a profit.

The formula will give you a rough "freeze price" the good-deal price that a sharp customer would pay, for the car. "Freeze price" means exactly what you might think— you have a set price in mind and you freeze at that price, not going up beyond it. It is a price for which, on the first try, you should be willing to walk out the door.

Your goal is to buy the car for the lowest price at which the dealer will sell it. The initial freeze price that I've been describing here is a freeze price that gives the dealer a minimum-profit deal. For many American cars, it is the price at which they will actually sell you the car. Some foreign cars can be bought at this initial freeze price as well.

Sometimes you will have to adjust your freeze price upward because you are trying to buy a car that is too desirable under current market conditions—a hard-to-find convertible, or an import that is benefiting from short supply and price-gouging sales managemant. Then maybe a couple of thousand extra is added to the base price of the car. Dealers with desirable cars to sell will raise their minimum-profit requirements on a car from $500 to $2,500 or even more when they know they can get away with it. Adjusting your freeze price should only be done cautiously, using the techniques discussed in the section "Hard to Get Cars." Remember, salespeople will *always* try to convince you that your freeze price is too low, that the car you want is a hot one, that the market is different now and you must make a better offer. You shouldn't give up your initial freeze price until you have tested a couple of dealers by walking out the door on them. Only after this final test do you have evidence that you are legitimately faced with buying a hot car, or a car for which dealers have conspired to hold a high minimum profit.

If you want to be more exact about the dealer's costs, get a copy of *Edmund's New Car Prices*, a cheap paperback in your local bookstore. *Edmund's* will give you a dealer cost figure for the car you want and for every factory-installed option, listed side by side with the suggested price you see on the sticker. Add up all those dealer's cost numbers for the options on your car, and the base figure for the car itself, and then add $600 to get your freeze price.

What if the new car you're buying is one of last year's models? (In other words, you're buying a 1987 model after the 1988 models have come out.) If the car you want has been "last year's car" for less than two months, subtract an additional 5 percent from the factory sticker. If it's been more than two months since the next year's cars have appeared, subtract 10 percent.

What if you're buying a demonstrator, or demo, a "new" car that has 500 or more miles on it from being driven around as a salesman's personal car? Take off 2 percent for each 500 miles on the odometer, but realize that the manager may well be hoping to sell the demo to another customer at more or less regular price.

So, take your freeze price, remember to say no to all the dealer-installed options and all the attempts at fraud and trickery that are described in this book. And there you have it, a great deal!

Now, for those of you who would like a bit more of an explanation, I will try to undo the confusion that auto dealers have created about the price of a car. In fact, there are eight different prices you have to consider:

1. *The Dealer's Asking Price.* Outrageous! This is the original factory sticker, plus maybe a second add-on sticker with phony charges for rustproofing, additional dealer markup, and so on.

2. *The Total Swindle Price.* Otherwise known as "the chart," this price is the total amount of money paid by a customer who is swindled in every way possible by the dealer. The customer who signs the chart buys the car at the full dealer's asking price, pays the top rate of interest on the financing, buys rustproofing, credit life insurance, and all the other bogus extras at the highest price charged by the dealer, and also gives away his trade-in for the lowest possible amount. A customer who falls for the total swindle can lose more than $5,000 compared to the customer who gets the minimum-profit deal, described below.

3. *The Factory Sticker Price.* This price is on the first sticker pasted on the window. By federal law, the factory sticker price will be identical for all cars of this type that have exactly the same equipment. You don't have to pay these prices, of course; it is just a place for

the lies to get started. The sticker is helpful since it allows you to calculate *your* price on the car.

4. *The Full Invoice Price.* In theory, this price is what the dealer paid for the car, plus charges to the dealer for freight and advertising. It includes a secret rebate to the dealer of at least 3 percent and sometimes more. The full invoice is about $500 over the base invoice, described below.

5. *The Base Invoice Price.* In theory, what the dealer paid for the car itself, though it always includes the secret rebate to the dealer of 3 percent or more.

6. *The True Cost of the Car.* This is the well-guarded secret of how much the dealer pays for the car. The true cost is the price on the full invoice, minus the secret rebate of 3 percent or more, plus a certain cost to the dealer of about two dollars a day for "renting" the car until it's sold.

7. *The Minimum-Profit Deal.* This is the well-guarded secret of the minimum price for which the dealer will sell the car. In ordinary cases, this is the full invoice price plus about $150. With the dealer's 3 percent rebate, this leaves a minimum profit to the dealer of more than $500 on a $12,000 car. The minimum-profit deal is unavailable when the dealer is confident of selling his car quickly to another customer at a higher price.

8. *What the Customer Pays for a Car.* Often has no connection to any of the above. After reading this book, it should be as close to the minimum-profit deal as possible.

As you can see, there's lots of room for these bums to confuse you. When you start thinking about new car prices, the place you should start is the sticker. By federal law, each new car must have the sticker, which gives the manufacturer's suggested retail price (MSRP) for the car and its options as it was completed at the factory.

When people say sticker price, they are usually referring to the original factory sticker. Dealers have been confusing things in recent years by putting a second sticker on the car, the add-on sticker, which lists dealer-installed options, rustproofing, or even items as bogus as "additional dealer markup," a marketing trick to make you think that the second sticker is as official as the first sticker. Thus they hope to convey the false impression that items such as rustproofing are already part of the car, and that you have no choice but to pay something close to the price at the bottom of that second sticker. The second-sticker routine is a very successful trick that has earned millions for the dealers who use it. This second sticker, as I've said above, is virtually pure profit and can in many cases be negotiated away altogether.

Getting back to the original factory sticker, note carefully the word "suggested" in "manufacturer's suggested retail price." That should tip you off that the price on the factory sticker is much more than the dealer paid for the car, often thousands more. On a typical American car the dealer has paid between $600 and $2000 less than the price on the factory sticker for the privilege of being able to sell the car to you.

How do dealers pay for the cars? Actually, modern car dealers, for the most part, don't "buy" their cars. They "rent" them from the manufacturers by paying interest on them—from Ford or Chrysler or whomever—until they sell them to you, at which time the dealer pays up his "lease" and keeps his share of the profit. That's why dealers are anxious to sell the cars they have: every day a car is on the lot, the dealer loses money. I use the word "loses" rather loosely, because there is so much profit in auto sales that many dealers are millionaires.

Aside from the price on the factory sticker, the "suggested" price, there is another price, the "invoice price," which theoretically represents how much the dealer pays for the car. However, even the concept of the "invoice price" is a bit fuzzy, because:

1. There's more than one kind of invoice. There's the *base invoice*, which represents the "cost" the car and its options as produced at factory, and the *full invoice*, which is the base invoice, plus the cost of

freight and dealer participation in advertising, charges billed from the manufacturer to the dealer;

2. The invoice price itself includes a profit to the dealer in the form of a rebate of about 3 percent, which the manufacturer will send back to the dealer after you have bought the car.

Dealers get a lot of mileage out of never admitting that such rebates exist ("Look, the invoice is all money we have to pay the manufacturer!") and by confusing the full invoice with the base invoice, thus getting you to pay for the freight charge twice.

The base invoice price is published in various books—notably *Edmund's New Car Prices* (Edmund Publications Corp., revised several times a year, editions for both American and foreign cars), available in many bookstores and libraries.

On typical American cars sticker-price markup is about 15 percent, or almost one-sixth, of the total (12 percent on some smaller cars, and 20 percent on some larger ones). The same is true of foreign cars, though they tend to vary more often from the norm. Somewhere in every car dealer's file cabinet, there is, accordingly, an invoice that shows, in this rough way, what the dealer paid for a car. Sometimes the dealer will even offer to show you the invoice to influence your negotiations. It looks easy, you might say: just add a reasonable profit to the invoice price, and you know how to get a good deal. But remember:

1. The invoice price includes an extra layer of profit, about 3 percent ($300 on a $10,000 car), which is rebated from the car manufacturer to the car dealer;

2. The full invoice already includes a freight or destination charge for shipping the car, of about $350, and a charge for dealer participatory advertising of about $100, so don't allow the dealer to bill you for them twice.

3. Crooked car dealers tend to keep fake invoices on hand to deal with customers who want to see the invoice.

The dealer will lie to you about the 3 percent rebate. He'll say that the invoice is all cost, and that's why he needs to get a big profit over the invoice to pay his electricity bill.

Here's a list to clarify what a dealer pays for a typical, new car:

Consider a new American car with a *factory sticker* of		$12,000:
Invoice price = 85% of *Sticker*	=	$10,200
(cost of car plus cost of options at factory)		
To this we add $450, as follows:		
Freight charge	=	$ 350
Advertising charge	=	$ 100
With these added, we get the *full invoice price*	=	$10,650
To get the *dealer cost*, we have to substract the		
dealer's 3% rebate given by the manufacturer	=	$ 360
leaving a *dealer cost* of	=	$10,290
So, *dealer cost* = 82% of STICKER [85%–3%] + $450	=	$10,290.
Also to be remembered is the *interest charge*,		
about $2 for every day the car is on the lot.		
Now, the *minimum profit for the dealer* is		
the *dealer's rebate* plus $150: ($360 + $150)	=	$ 510
Your *best minimum deal* on a new car is the		
dealer cost ($10,290)		
plus his *minimum profit* ($510), which is	=	$10,800
So: *dealer cost* = 82% of STICKER + $450	=	$10,290
minimum profit = 3% of STICKER + $150		510
your best deal = 85% of STICKER + $600	=	$10,800

That's pretty much how it works. This is not an exact guide, however. The cost of some American cars can be as low as 80 percent of the sticker price and as high as 88 percent, as opposed to the 85 percent mentioned above. The interest charge is usually too confusing for even managers to reckon. (How long has that damn car been on this lot?) Note that the $150 + invoice deal is much more than $150 profit becuase of the 3 percent rebate. (Dealers like to pretend the invoice is all cost and that only the money over the invoice is profit.)

It's not simple, is it? A lot of salesmen don't understand it, either. They just know, roughly, what the sharpest customers can bargain down as a discount on a new car.

And there are still more variables to control here. For one thing, to be accurate about profit margins, you should use the most recent edition of *Edmund's Car Prices*. More confusingly, sometimes the manufacturer will give some kind of secret incentive to the dealer—"4 percent rebates instead of 3 percent on all the X-cars you sell," the manufacturer might say. That's an extra $100 bucks a car or so. The manager might say at a sales meeting, "A $20 bonus to every salesman who sells an X-car this month!" But you, the customer, won't know about this "special," or the fact that you could negotiate for a share of that extra X-car profit.

The salesman himself will get one-fourth to one-third of the total profit on the car sale, which can be $3,000 or more. For example, on a $15,000 car:

Full sticker price includes 15% profit ($2,250), minus charges for freight, etc. ($450)	$1,800
3% rebate	$ 450
Rustproofing, fabric protection	$ 995
Additional dealer markup	+ $ 395
	$3,640

So, thus far the profit is $3640, with a cool grand in the salesman's pocket. Now if the finance guy sells the customer credit life insurance, accident and health insurance, an extended service plan, and financing of a $10,000 car loan at three points over the market rate, these items could add up to a profit margin of $1,260
Plus perhaps they undervalued the customer's trade-in by $ 600
This would leave a profit margin to the dealership of $5,500

Now, no one is questioning the dealer's right to make a profit. But notice that though the customer could have bought the car for $150 over invoice (leaving the dealer with a profit of $600, and about $150 in the salesman's pocket), the dealer made more than *nine times* that amount through the various schemes detailed in this book. You can see how it works—rustproofing, credit life insurance, it all sounds so sensible, doesn't it? Even a customer who fights tooth and nail with the above figures, and bargains them down a couple of thousand, could still be spending $3,000 more than necessary.

Now you know why some people are so happy to be in the car business. Now you know why there's so much money to be made. Now you know better.

Understanding the Minimum-profit Deal

The "minimum profit" deal on a car, in general, is about $150 over full invoice, the invoice including freight and advertising. As explained above, $150 over invoice usually gives the dealer a profit of about $500 because of the 3 percent rebate he will get from the factory on the invoice price itself.

I can't be more exact than this because neither are the dealers. The $150 over full invoice will put you in the very close range of the ultimate car deal. The way to be sure of getting to the bottom is to negotiate hard: bang on their heads and see how low they will go.

On the average American car—this is a good rule of thumb—the base invoice is 15 percent below the factory sticker. On some small cars it can be as low as 12 percent; on some of the large luxury cars it is 20 percent. But the broad midrange of cars will have a 15 percent markup. Moreover, the markup is greater on the factory-installed options. The base car might have a markup of 12 percent, but then the air conditioning, automatic transmission, and the rest will have markups of 18 percent, averaging out to 15 percent. If you have a car with a lot of factory options, you have a bigger profit margin that you can negotiate.

Foreign cars are less fixed in their profit margins, because here we're playing with variables such as exchange rates and the price supports of foreign governments. But the range is still usually between 12 and 20 percent, and the 15 percent rule of thumb figure is average. In the early 1980s, some of the imports were so popular that dealers didn't sell them near the level of minimum profit, but hundreds or even thousands of dollars above it. This trend continued into the mid-1980s, though many customers find they can still get a rare bargain by pressing hard for a low price.

To repeat, a typical good deal is:

Base invoice + $450 + $150; or
Base invoice + $600; or
Full invoice + $150

This is the formula to use if you are employing the detailed statistics of *Edmund's Car Prices. Edmund's* will enable you to add up the total base invoice price; so just add $600 and you've got your freeze price.

The base invoice, as I have said, is usually about 15 percent off of sticker, so we can also start the calculation with the

Factory sticker price
Subtract 15%
Add $600

Use this formula if you don't have *Edmund's* with you. It will bring you within a few dollars, in many cases, of the correct minimum deal. (For small cars or cars with few factory options, the margin is about 12 percent, and on top-of-the-line models it can approach 20 percent.)

When you are negotiating, the salesman may try to charge you the freight charge more than once. If you agree to pay him $600 above "cost," he'll show you an invoice and add $600 even though the invoice he showed you already included the freight charge. Remember: $150 above full invoice (freight, etc. included), or $600 above base invoice. (Don't forget the possibility that the dealership might create a phony invoice with their photocopy machine.)

Are you entirely confused now? It really is a mess, and the car dealers want to make sure it *stays* a mess so that the customer is as confused as possible. For purposes of actually buying the car, you can always go back to the simple formula I gave you at the beginning of this chapter.

Wheeling and Dealing in the New Car Showroom

It's funny how even the ads for car dealers mention it. "Come on in and make your best deal!" It's as if dealing were some mystical process with an uncertain result. Actually, if the ads were accurate, they'd say something like, "Come on in and listen to the lies we'll tell you! See how many of them you believe! We're pretty persuasive, but even if you don't believe all our lies, we'll still sell you a car!"

There's no real trick to negotiating a car other than being in control of the numbers (i.e., knowing a good discount when you see it) and resisting the lies salespeople tell you. Car dealers would like you to believe car sales is like a garage sale. "How much you wanna give me? Two bucks? Fifty cents? Sure, I'll take it." They love the people who just like to deal without really knowing the prices: you go up, they come down, you go up again, they maybe come down a little. They make their fortunes from customers who don't know what a good deal is and who mistakenly believe it's fair to give some extra money to the dealer above the first offer. "After all, we've come down a little, so you can go up a little."

Some customers like the idea of the straightforward freeze price. You offer the dealer your freeze price, and keep on saying no to his requests for more money. If he doesn't give in, you walk out the door; if he doesn't chase after you, you buy the car somewhere else at that freeze price.

It works sometimes, but I have found it psychologically easier for car dealers to give me the right price if I make my first offer several hundred dollars *below* the freeze price. That way they can feel they "succeeded" in bargaining me up a few hundred, making it psychologically easier for them to sign the deal. Their egos aren't happy unless they think they got something out of you, or "bumped" you up in price, as they say, so I give them that pleasure in exchange for them giving me the car at the right price. Usually I will go up three or four times. If the freeze price on a car is $8,300, I will make my first offer at $7,900, a second at $8,100, a third at $8,250 and finally yield at $8,300.

You have to show you're serious about buying the car; salespeople are suspicious of customers who are just fishing for prices; they are reluctant to reveal just how low they will go to such customers. That's why it helps to pretend you're a naive person (more vulnerable to impulse, on-the-spot purchases); it helps to pretend that this is the first car dealer you've visited (shows you're not shopping for prices, and that maybe you are ready to buy a car); and to be confident that you can afford the car and that you are ready to take it home *today* (so they can put their full energy into making a serious deal for you).

One of the ways I tease the dealer is by giving him a deposit check during the negotiations. Car dealers like to get a deposit from you—they think that if you have written a $1,000 check to the dealer, you are already hooked on the car. They trust that you are scared to leave the dealer without your check (giving them more time to hammer on you), and that you are vulnerable to being "bumped" on the price of the car.

I often spook them by offering a check or credit card with my first or second offer on a car. This shows them concrete evidence that I am a serious buyer. You can see them salivate with the prospect of having a real sale in their hands. They might think they control me by having my check, but I know that I get the check back if I don't take the car, and that they will hate to blow the deal after things have gone along so far. The deposit check shows I am serious, and often induces them to give in to the freeze price I have specified.

If you want to feel totally safe while you are teasing them with money, put your car deposit on your credit card. That way, if you don't take the car home, Visa or whoever cannot bill the charge to you. It's that simple.

Remember—this cannot be stressed enough—they will not think you are serious about your low price until you show you are willing to walk away from the car if you don't get it. You must be prepared to walk away, and look sincere about it. Take some time before you walk away so that they know you are not just fishing for prices and that you really want to buy the car. Argue with them for a few minutes. When you do walk, walk slowly, give them a chance to swallow their pride and come after you with another offer. If you aren't willing to walk, they will often remain there, silently, waiting for you to come up in price. It's pure bluff. You've got to be ready to walk.

You may be wondering, "What kinds of things do I say to the salesman?" Actually, it's quite easy because the salesman will do most of the talking. You just have to stick to your freeze price, and say, "No, I really want to buy the car at the price I've mentioned," as many times as necessary. Other than that, just be friendly and chatty. Be friendly even if you're walking out the door. It may influence them to give in.

Maybe the hardest thing about negotiating a car is letting your reason keep control of your emotions. It's such a hassle that you're tempted to end it quickly, even at the cost of losing hundreds of dollars. You want the car so badly, and the salesman has it, and it seems like he won't give it to you unless you agree to his price. You are tempted to give in because you might feel defeated if you go home without the car. As I've said, before you can win a car at a good price you must show the salesman that you are willing to walk if the price is not right. If you feel in any way as if the encounter has slipped out of your control and you are in danger of getting a bad deal, or you are just too tired and overwrought about the whole thing, go home and come back tomorrow. Remember, the same deal will be there for you, despite what the salesman says.

The upper hand is *always* yours. You have the money, and the pressure is on them because you are ready to buy today. If things aren't worked out your way, the salesman will have to explain to the boss how he blew a deal—remember that.

Hot Cars That Cost More

As I said at the beginning of this book, you should buy the exact car that you want. On many cars, especially many American cars, you can get a great bargain. Ultimately, though, the right car for you is not the cheapest car but the car that makes your heart throb, the car that meets your needs and fulfills your desires. Sometimes the car you really want is also a car that a lot of other people really want, and the dealer will not let it go for a minimum profit because he is sure he can sell it at a much higher price to someone else.

If this seems to be the case, I want you to think about these things. First of all, is the car you want really worth the extra money? I don't mean worth it in general, but rather personally, for you, is it worth it? If you're wealthy and money doesn't matter, I think it is perfectly fine to get the exact toy you want. If you aren't wealthy, but you have a little extra money and you would like to spend that on the car of your dreams, that's fine, too, as long as you are realistic. You must be able to say to yourself, "I am passing up these other pleasures and goods because I am spending my extra money on car payments for the particular car I wanted." If you're still comfortable with that, then you should go ahead and get that car.

Also consider whether you are really enchanted with the car you have in mind or are just seduced by the social image of it. Do you really like the car, or do you just think you do because other people like it? Is it the kind of car you think you should have to complete your social image? If you still want the car after asking these questions, then you can reasonably prepare to buy that especially expensive car.

Also worth considering is if something more inexpensive might fulfill the same needs; for example, a vehicle that is also a sports car, but costs $6,000 less. You may want a convertible, but you might realize you would be just as happy with the fresh air of an open sun roof.

Examine the possibility that you are captive to brand loyalty. Is it possible you have such fond memories of your old Beetle that you now refuse to buy anything but another Volkswagen? Many car buyers are loyal to their old brand, regardless of other cars that might better serve their needs. Every manufacturer changes over the years—for example, VW doesn't make Beetles anymore—so try being open-minded to other cars that might be easier to obtain and therefore cheaper.

All right, you tell me, you still want that hard-to-get Japanese car, or that convertible that no dealer in town seems to keep in stock. How do you negotiate the price?

First of all, you must be initially skeptical of the salesman's comments. *"These cars are selling like hotcakes! You're lucky to get the last one in this color! My, it's a pretty one. We'd sell it tomorrow if you weren't buying it today!"* Salesmen are trained to say this sort of thing to build the value of the car in your mind and make you willing to fork over more money for it. So don't swallow what they say at face value.

Even if the car is in some demand, you can count on

the salesman to exaggerate it. *"We've had dealers from four states call us and beg us to ship this car to them!"* Any lie to enhance the profit margin—that's the salesman's golden rule.

It is important to remember that there is very, very rarely a car that can't be bargained down at least a little. Even if a car is so hot that it is selling at a high price, dealers will put a still *higher* price on the car, hoping that someone will be willing to pay it. But most cars have some room for bargaining for a customer who is willing to buy it now: dealers will always prefer to sell a car now rather than tomorrow, and they will usually give a discount for this opportunity.

Particularly among people who sell Japanese cars, I have noticed a very strong attempt to put over the lie that there is nothing to be negotiated. *"Toyotas are selling like hotcakes! We can't keep 'em on the lot! That's right, our price is $3,000 over sticker. Take it or leave it."* It's true that Japanese cars were popular at the same time as supplies were limited by early-1980s import quotas, and dealers were able to sell much of their inventory without discounting. But salesmen of Japanese cars have silently colluded in conveying the impression that there is just no negotiating the price, ever. "It's a great value, ma'am, I'm sure you'll agree, for this kind of quality." You must be careful to demonstrate that you will seriously buy if the price can be bargained, otherwise you are walking.

But the big question is, how do you bargain for a car that is selling for more than the minimum-profit deal? How do you know what is the correct freeze price? How do you know when the salesmen are telling the truth in their declarations that they won't sell the car for less? How do you know when they aren't lying anymore?

The answer is in the false buy, where you pretend to be a serious customer but are actually shopping for prices. When a car is selling at a premium and dealers won't go for a minimum-profit deal, the only way to find a good deal is through several false buys on a car. You must go shopping for the car, and you must pretend to be a customer with cash in hand ready to buy today. You must seem sincere, or else salespeople won't lower the price for you. You must hold out for a low figure, walk out the door, and see if they chase after you. If you have the chance to try this at two or three dealers for a similar car, the terms of a really good deal will become clear. The only way to fish for prices is to pretend to be a serious car buyer—there really isn't any other way. It is important to overcome your fear of contradicting yourself, too, because after testing a dealer on a price by walking out the door, you may want to come back in and buy the car once you have determined that the price is reasonable.

Often you will get the true low price as you are in the parking lot ready to drive away and leave. The salesman will yell through your window, "If I could get you that car for $10,500, would you buy it?" This is called a "lowball," and hints strongly at the actual discount available to you. Don't be shy about coming back, but demand that they deliver what their lowball offer promised! As I've said above, salespeople aren't ashamed of lying to you over and over again, so you shouldn't be ashamed of changing your mind repeatedly and coming back to buy the car.

This is the point when shopping for a car can be very time-consuming. But a series of false buys is the only way to find out the accurate discount on that convertible or pricey import that you want. A hassle? Maybe. But how much hassle is it worth to save $1,000 or $2,000? If you look at it as a game, you can even enjoy it. You're there, a phony customer, going "undercover," just as I did to research this book. You're out there trying to find out how low they will go in discounting a Zargon Cream Puff convertible. The only way you'll find out is by asking for a big discount, protesting that you can't buy a car without one, and eventually walking out the door to see if they will chase after you with a better offer. If your time at one dealer hasn't satisfied you that you have arrived at a true rock-bottom discount, you can try the same at two or three other dealers until eventually the correct freeze price emerges. At each new dealer you must pretend to be a fresh customer, which means you must patiently wait while the salesman shows you the same car again. But your payoff will be the money you save, by finding either the true discount or a dealer who discounts more than the others. Good luck!

Your Trade-in

It's often best to sell your old car privately. You'll get a slightly better price than the "wholesale" price a dealer would pay you. This, of course, can be a hassle, and puts you to the trouble of waiting to find a buyer for your old car.

Many people gauge the value of their old car with one of the books that list used car prices. Such books are helpful, but they can also help you lose hundreds of dollars if you sell to a car dealer.

If you let a car dealer know you have consulted the *Blue Book* (or whatever) or your trade-in, he has a ready-made pack of lies about why the book you looked at is out of date, or doesn't apply to the area where you live, or why the market for your car has changed, or why your car has lots of things wrong with it to make the value even lower. Another disaster, which happens more often than you might suppose, is that your car's market value is more than that listed in the book. This is true when and where there is a shortage of good late-model used cars.

The only way to find out the true wholesale value of your trade-in is to take it shopping at a few used car outlets. Take it to at least four. Make one of them an established used car dealer, and another a new car dealer with a used car department. If you want to be really funny, take it to the used car department of the car dealer at which you will later shop for a new car.

Tell each of these dealers that you would like to sell your used car, you are shopping it to three or four places, and you will sell it to the one that gives you the best offer. The used car guys are sharp about cars, often as sharp as they are about deceiving customers. If they think you can be fooled by a low figure, they will give it to you. But for the most part, they are interested in getting some good inventory, and most of them will give you a realistic figure. If the several dealers are in the same ballpark, you know you've got the price. If they differ wildly, you know you need to take your car to a few more.

Take the highest figure you get (if it is reasonable, not wildly above all the others), and demand that price from the new car dealer for your trade-in. But don't let him withhold any of the discount you negotiated on the new car!

When you're negotiating for a new car and trading in the old one, dealers will take this time as an opportunity to confuse you. They'll try to fudge the new car price and the old car price so that it isn't clear what the difference is. They'll talk to you about "allowance figures" and "difference prices," but you just relax, take it nice and slow. Insist that they keep it all clear before you.

"How much are you giving me for my old car?" When they get to a figure that you're happy with, you can ask: "How much is my discount on the new car?" When the new car price is all set, check the way they add and subtract! Add it up yourself five times if you have to. The great mathematicians of the world often add things up two or three times just to be sure they're right. Especially at car dealers! For example, the new car you want to buy has a factory sticker price of $12,000. Your freeze price on this car is $10,800, which you figure as follows:

New car price	$12,000
Subtract 15%	−$ 1,800
Base invoice price	$10,200
Add $600 (freight, etc. + $150)	$10,800

Now, you also have a trade-in. After shopping your car at several used car dealers, you find you have a used car worth $3,900. By trading the car to the new car dealer, your price should be $6,900, as follows:

Freeze price on new car	$10,800
True value of trade-in	−$ 3,900
Your final cost ("difference")	$ 6,900

As you can see, there is plenty of room here for salesmen to confuse people by writing down wrong numbers. So triple-check the numbers; and if you still aren't sure, copy the numbers down and take them home to look over before you sign the deal.

It's Not Final until You Take the Car Away

It's true. It doesn't matter what you've signed, how much deposit money you've given them, or anything else. If you haven't driven the car away, the deal's not complete. One time the dealer I was working for had a problem with people who were shocked by the finance guy's fraud tricks. One of the customers ran out of the finance office—even though he had already signed for the car—and wanted to go home. "You chase after him and calm him down!" ordered the manager. "But, boss," the salesman said, "he already signed the buyer's order. And he gave us a deposit." "That's nothing," said the manager. "If he doesn't take the car home, there's nothing we can do to enforce that deal. You get him and drag him back in here and make him take that car!"

It's true that your signature is significant. If you do take the car home *after* you've signed, it's legal evidence that you bought the car. But if the dealer has been playing fraud tricks on you, or if you've just become unsure of what's going on, stop and refuse to take the car home. Even if they say they've got your trade-in locked up. They've got to give it back. Tell them you'll take a taxi and sue.

This is important to know, too, in case there's something wrong with the car that they haven't fixed. Let's say during the test drive that the wipers didn't work. While you were signing papers they promised to put in a new wiper mechanism. The paperwork's all done, they hand you the car. You try the wipers, they don't work. *Don't take the car home.* "I'm sorry, ma'am, the service department is closed. You can bring it back any morning next week and we'll have those wipers fixed in a jiffy." Maybe they will, maybe they won't. But if you refuse to take the car, they will work very hard to make sure that any problems you've noted are taken care of immediately. The deal is not official, not complete, not put on their profit sheets until you take delivery of your car. Delivery means your taking the car home after the papers have been signed. Then, and only then, is your contract with the dealer completely in effect.

However, if you bring the car back in two or three days and say that it doesn't work right, you're usually within your legal rights to get your money back.

9

Financing Your Car

Have you ever thought about what a funny concept "financing" is? Today, instead of just "borrowing money," as you did in the old days, you "get financed." Or the salesman says, "Don't worry, we'll get you some financing," as if it were a cup of coffee to help you through the day. You pay a lot of money for the privilege of being financed, yet you often feel as if the dealer is doing you a favor.

Most of us borrow money when we buy a car these days. Even people who have the cash get car loans so they don't have all their money tied up in a car. Even if you happen to have enough cash to make the entire payment up front, you may find that dealers will encourage you to finance your car anyway—dealers get kickbacks from certain finance companies. With cars being as expensive as they are, however, it's not easy for most of us to buy a car without financing.

It's important to do your financing in a smart way; otherwise you can lose a good deal of money. What follows is everything you need to know to finance your car intelligently.

How Much Can I Afford to Finance?

You, of course, know your own income and how much cash you have in the bank. You know, too, that the more cash you put down on the car, the less you will have to finance, and the lower your monthly payments will be.

You may have some equity, in other words, cash value, in the form of an older car you are going to sell or trade in when you buy your new car. (If you still owe money on your old car, see below.)

Second, you may have some cash in the bank that you are willing to spend for a down payment on a car. (If you don't have such money, don't worry. As the salesmen say, "We'll take care of you.") You may wonder, "Is it better to have cash in the bank, or make a bigger down payment on a car?" I think this is just personal preference. Do you want the money in hand so you can splurge on a trip to Europe, or would you rather have lower monthly payments and a greater cash value in your car? Do what feels right for *you*.

Third, once you consider the cash value of your old car, and the cash you are going to give as a down payment, you will be borrowing the rest in a car loan. How much car can you buy? This depends both on the interest rate and the length of the car loan. Today, the typical car loan is for a four- or five-year period. (You can still get three-year car loans, though the monthly payment will be higher; and seven-year loans are possible for cars costing over $20,000.) The amount of car you can buy for your monthly payment obviously depends on the interest rate, too. For standard car loans of four and five years, the following is a guide to how much you will have to pay, per month, for every $1,000 you borrow:

	4 years	5 years
10%	$25.37	$21.25
12%	$26.34	$22.25
14%	$27.33	$23.27

So if you want a $10,000 car loan and current new car loans have interest rates of 12 percent, your monthly payment should be 10 × $26.34, or $263.40. You can make it a rough rule of thumb: $25 a month for every $1,000 you want to borrow for the car.

There is more than one way to calculate interest, but these days the law is insisting that interest rates be presented to you in the form of an annual percentage rate (APR). When discussing interest rate, make sure it is put in terms of APR.

Obviously, things can get pretty complicated here; if you are financing $13,245 at a percentage rate of 11.25, what's your monthly payment? Things can get tricky, but just make sure the financing papers include two things: the amount being financed (the amount you are borrowing), and the interest rate in APR. Make sure, too, that salespeople haven't thrown in any other items such as credit life insurance on the financing form. But you can generally trust the arithmetic. If they multiplied wrong, they can go to jail. Car dealers will try every lie and fraud possible, but they will not do any tricks on paper that could serve as evidence against them. The math will always be correct: what you need to check are the figures they supplied. (Is that really what I agreed to pay for the car? Hey, I didn't want any rustproofing! I didn't want the extended service contract, either!)

Five-Year Car Loans

Car loans used to be for two or three years, and the four-year car loan was a big deal. Today, cars are expensive, and we Americans don't care how long we're in debt. The main point is a lower monthly payment, right? So what if a car becomes a bucket of bolts in five years? For example, if you borrow $10,000 at 12 percent, a four-year car loan has a monthly payment of $263.34, and a five-year car loan has a monthly payment of $222.45. That sounds a lot better, doesn't it?

Seriously, I think five-year car loans are a great idea. If you really do want a lower monthly payment, and your desire for a lower payment is making you think about leasing, I'd definitely prefer the five-year car loan to leasing.

One catch is that the banks are slightly more nervous

about five-year car loans, partly because of how little the car is worth at the end of five years, but mostly because the first year or two of payments are mostly interest rather than principal. If you didn't put much money down, you have little or none of your own equity or cash value in the car for a long time.

They way banks express their nervousness is by charging slightly higher interest rates for five-year loans. (This also is a function of their estimate of the economic forecast over five years.) So in borrowing $10,000 for a car, your choice might be four years at 12 percent ($263.34 per month), or five years at 13 percent ($227.54 per month). The five years still sound good.

Where Should I borrow the Money?

Sometimes your credit union will have the best terms on a car loan. If you don't belong to a credit union, your bank or savings and loan association is often the most economical source for borrowing the money. It pays to shop around at different banks for interest rates, because they can vary by two points or more in the same town at the same time. Many banks will be happy to give you a car loan even though you don't have an account there. You can often apply for the car loan before you go to the dealer (just keep in mind the kind of car you want to buy and the amount you want to borrow.) So when you go to the dealer, you can already have an approved loan to make you feel more confident. A word of caution: banks will try to sell you useless credit life insurance, just like the finance guy at the car dealer!

The finance guy at the car dealer will usually be happy to lend you money. "Step right over here, ma'am, and we'll get you financed!" They'll always try to do it at a higher interest rate, too. But there are some good reasons to use dealer financing:

1. If your new car is a lemon, you can stop payments to a dealer's finance company.

2. A dealer will finance you for little or no money down, whereas a bank might require as much as one-quarter of the price of the car as a down payment.

3. If your credit is marginal or bad, the dealer has the power to "kiss the paper" and get you financed anyway.

Dealer financing is almost always offered to you at a rate higher than the bank's. Unlike a bank, however, a car dealer is one place where the finance rate is negotiable. It's rather like the car negotiation, in that you simply hold out for the lower rate. You may feel shy about doing this if your credit is marginal. You might be thinking, "I'm glad they lent me the money at all." But if they're giving you credit, they can certainly offer it to you at a respectable rate. Big outfits like GMAC or Chrysler Credit can get money near the prime rate and millions of dollars of it. They make a profit on just about every financing, so there's no need to make an outrageous profit from you.

When you are negotiating for financing, the finance guy may say, "I'm sorry, our financing is at 16 percent. If you want a lower rate, you should go to the bank. We merely provide financing as a convenience for our customers, but we're under no obligation to be competitive." He may be too lazy to take the trouble to write up the loan forms for you, or he may be trying to keep a high "average financing rate" to earn a bonus, and therefore refuse to get you financed. But you still have a card to play.

The finance guy works for the car dealer, even though he might act like he has a separate empire. If you want (or need) dealer financing and you want it at a competitive rate, you can still refuse to take the car. You can say, "I'm sorry, but I'm just not taking the car home unless I get financing at a competitive rate, and I want the financing from you." Force the finance guy to talk to the general manager—you'll get results.

Even if you've signed the papers for buying the car, you aren't obligated to take the car home, regardless of what they say. Your legal position is strong. The dealer knows that he cannot enforce the sales contract if you don't drive the car away. Obviously the contract can't be complete until the financing is worked out.

So it is important that you not take the car home until everything is complete, with the car working perfectly and the financing all written up to your liking. If it is late in the evening, the dealer will try to get you to take the new car home and say, "We'll work out the financing tomorrow." You should always refuse. Although the deal would not be fully binding, you're in a stickier situation if you've already begun to treat the car like it's yours.

Establishing Your Credit

At one point or another in the financing process, you are asked to fill out a credit application. I recommend a reasonable amount of honesty. Lying to get credit is a crime; moreover, credit people are fairly good at judging how much you can pay, and will often lend you as much or more money than you can reasonably handle.

I don't think it's a good idea to get in over your head on car payments. But even if you know you can afford the payments, it's important to fill out the credit application in the proper manner.

Be reasonably thorough in filling out the forms. Remember that the image you want to project is that of a stable person with a good stable job and a regular income. So, when they ask you how long you've lived somewhere, don't say "two months", say "first year." Sounds better already, doesn't it? Personal references, family and otherwise, are important. If you don't have family, put some close friends down as "cousins." If you plan on moving soon, or plan on quitting your job and getting another, *don't* let them know. You may know that you will always have enough money to make the payments, but you've got to convince them of that. Don't be too ready to admit all the times you've moved, or all the times you've changed jobs. These questions leave people room to fib a bit.

In addition, finance people will run a credit-bureau check using your social security number, and call your employer to verify your job and income. A tremendous hint: if you have a problem with your job or employer, buy your car on an evening or a Saturday when they can't make a phone check with your boss. Car dealers can always wrap up the deal on the spot. If everything looks good, they will let you take the car home. If they are hesitant, insist that you take home the car now, or else you will be shopping at another dealer. "I hate hassles," you can tell them. "I want to wrap things up in one visit, or maybe I'll see if some other dealer has a better deal."

Nearly every dealer has a credit-bureau computer, which will call up a lot of your recent history—previous car loans, department-store charges, all that kind of stuff. Don't worry if your credit history is not perfect, they know you're only human. Have an explanation ready for the finance guy. *"I was really ill for three months, that's why I missed the payments to Bozo's furniture store." "The product was no good; I kept on trying to return it, but they slammed my credit rating instead."* Your credit rating is a precious thing. Protect it so you can borrow more money later on. Your recent credit history is the most important, however. If you need to build up your credit to buy a car later this year, take some kind of a small loan, even on a department-store credit card, and pay it back faithfully. Then you can show the car finance guy how well you've been doing.

Although the amount you borrow in a car loan is large, you can get car loans relatively easily for two reasons. First of all, unlike many consumer loans, your car loan is tied to a prime piece of collateral—your car. If you don't make the payments, the lender gets the car back. A used car is not worth as much as a new car, of course, and that's why lenders like you to make a down payment—if they have to "repo" (repossess) the car, they won't lose so much money. Also, after you've put a lot of money into it, *you* will be less likely to give up your car unless you're really desperate.

Second, dealers are anxious to get you financed because if they don't finance you, they don't sell a car. So they will really bend over backward to get you financed. I have seen car dealers give financing to people with the most marginal credit. So never assume that you can't get car financing. The dealer will always be glad to try!

Trade-ins and the Bucket Problem

Things can get pretty complicated if you are not only financing a new car, but you *also* owe money on your old car. Obviously you need to get things *re*financed and get rid of your old car loan before you can get happily rolling in your new wheels.

A special problem here is the "bucket" problem. Although you have been making your payments regularly, you may still owe more money than your old car is worth. You're "in the bucket," as the dealers say.

"How can that be?," you ask. "How is it that I can be making payments on a car for many months, and yet still owe more than the value of the car?"

Well, you know, of course, that a new car loses a lot of its value as soon as you drive it off the lot. You buy a brand-new $10,000 car, but suppose you get sick of it the next day. You want to sell it. Can you get someone to give you $10,000 for it? No way! All you have is a "like new," very good used car. Sure, it's worth a lot. But no one is going to give you $10,000 for it. How much would you pay for a car that someone had bought new the week before? You probably wouldn't want it, and instead would pay a little extra to get a real new car from a dealer. You might take it only if it cost a lot less than the price of a brand-new one, only if it were, let's say, $1,000 less. So you see, a car goes down in value as soon as you drive it away.

Whether your old car was bought new or used, you may still be in the bucket, though being in the bucket is more likely with new cars. If you have a loan on the car, you can end the loan right away with a "payoff." A payoff is the amount of money it takes to cancel the loan, when you want to get rid of the loan immediately with one cash payment. The payoff is less than the total of monthly payments you have left because you won't have to pay any more interest if you make the payoff today. A big portion of those monthly payments is interest, but the payoff includes only the amount of principal that you owe. However, sometimes a payoff can cost you extra, because of financial penalties for ending the loan early. (The bank won't be making money from you on interest anymore, so sometimes it charges a penalty.) Whenever you have an old car loan and you're trying to buy a new car, you have to, in some way, arrange for the payoff of the old loan, or have the finance guy arrange it for you.

You should know, too, how most modern loans work. With most loans, the early payments are devoted mostly to interest and very little to principal. On a four-year car loan, the first two years are heavily weighted toward paying the interest, and only toward the end do the payments become weighted toward paying off the actual loan. On a 30-year mortgage on a house, the first 10 years are mostly interest. The banks like it that way because they make more money. (You've "borrowed" the principal for a longer time, so they charge you even more interest on it because it's not paid off until later.) It sounds awful, but that's the way they work.

You don't buy a new car for an investment. You buy a new car because it's fun and comes fresh from the factory. But you pay extra for it. The amount the car is worth at any given time is simply what someone else will pay you for it. When you are trading it in, you are considering its wholesale price—what a dealer would reasonably offer to you for it. The problem is, when you bought the car, you financed the price of a *new* car, which is much more than it will ever be worth again. If you didn't make a really big down payment, you could end up owing more than the car is worth.

You can also be in the bucket on a car that you bought used, if you paid more than the car was actually worth. Given that your first payments mostly go to interest and the value of the car is going down all the time, the fact that you paid much more than the car was worth because of the crooked car salesman could land you in the bucket.

You're in the bucket whenever the payoff (the amount it takes to cancel the loan) is more than the wholesale value of the car. In other words, you can't get rid of the car without *paying* somebody to take it! This can happen, as I've said, because of (a) the rapid depreciation of a car; (b) the inflated initial price you may have paid for a car; and (c) the imbalance in loan payments, whereby the early payments cover mostly interest rather than a reduction of the principal amount you owe.

So, when you're financing a new car, you may be faced with the bucket problem. How do you find out if you're in the bucket? Once again, don't take the salesman's word for it! Check with the people who hold your old car loan to find out what the payoff is. They'll let you know. Then, check out the value of your old car by taking it to used car dealers, as I've discussed previously. Tell them you want to sell the car, that you are shopping it at a few dealers, and that you will give it to the one who makes you the best offer. If what you owe is more than what you can get, congratulations! You're in the bucket!

If you still want a new car, you must simply accept the fact that you will have to borrow not only enough money to purchase your new car, after giving your down payment, but also enough money to get yourself out of the bucket on the old car.

Car dealers do this sort of thing all the time, so don't let them try to act like they're doing you a big favor for which you should pay extra. Clearly, with such complications, you've got to take the time to make sure things are straight. Here's an example:

My old car:	wholesale value	$ 3,900
	Payoff (to cancel loan)	$ 4,200
	Amount in the bucket	$ 300
New car I want to buy:	factory sticker price	$12,000
	Freeze price (what I will pay)	$10,800
minus	My down payment	$ 1,000
	Amount of new car to finance	$ 9,800

plus	Amount of bucket to finance	$ 300
minus	Value of trade	− $ 3,900
	amount to pay off old loan	+ $ 4,200
	Total amount to finance	$10,100

So, we've gotten you into a new car at a good price. But we had to borrow enough money to get you out of the bucket. Now that you've gotten your new car, of course, you're even deeper in the bucket. You owe even more money on a car that's worth less than what you owe. But you only live once, right?

You might be asking, "How do I stay out of the bucket? How do I stay out of the situation of owing more on my car than the actual value of the car?" The way to do it is by making large down payments (whether in the form of cash or trade-in), or by keeping your new cars for several years. If you buy a new car every year, each year you're going to wind up paying for the quick depreciation or decline in value of a new car. Remember, the new car becomes a used car as soon as you drive it away.

So, if it's your first new car and you make a small down payment, you'll be in the bucket. If you keep it for several years, though, you'll have enough equity (value) in your car, provided you haven't made a total wreck of it, to avoid the bucket on your next car if you keep your tastes reasonable.

Balloon Financing

An interesting way to lower your monthly payments is by the "balloon financing" method. A "balloon" is a large final payment at the end of the term of the loan. If you borrow $10,000 for a car the ordinary way, you will pay back the principal and interest in equal payments over four years.

With balloon financing, you have a big $3,000 payment due, all at once, at the end of the four-year period—that's the bad side. The good side is that your monthly payments over the four years will cover only $7,000, plus the interest on $7,000, plus the interest on the $3,000 balloon.

The benefit is low monthly payments. The drawback is a big balloon due in four years. How do you pay for the balloon? Either by selling or trading in the car before the four years are up, or by refinancing the balloon with your bank when the four years are up. Nobody really expects you to come up with $3,000 all of a sudden. The balloon is a helpful technique because it lets you own the car you want with a lower monthly payment. But be careful, because the dealer will use the "lower monthly payment" line to get you to pay a higher price for the car, a price you will eventually pay in the form of more interest and a bigger balloon. This translates into a much lower equity in the car when you trade it in or sell it.

Buying a New Car with No Money Down

It is reasonably easy to buy a brand-new car with no money down. It's a lot easier than buying real estate for no money down. If it thrills you to take home a new car just on your say-so, by all means go ahead and do it.

In fact, you can do what I did when I made my first deal for a new car—I bought a brand-new sports car with no cash, at a time when I didn't have a job. It isn't all that hard once you know what you're doing.

When you buy a new car with no money down, of course, you'll definitely be in the bucket: you'll owe more than the car is worth. But if you can make the payments, you plan to keep the car for a long time, and you'd like to have the transportation, it's worth going through with it. I *don't* urge you to buy a new car if you can't afford it. Buying a car with no money down is simply a financing technique for people who feel sure they can make the payments later. But it is awful to get your car repossessed, and you *do not want* that kind of damage done to your credit rating.

Remember that the dealer will do anything within reason to sell you a car. He's in business to sell cars, and if you let him know you'll only buy a car under certain circumstances, he'll consider whatever you want. If you say you'll buy the car only if you don't have to pay cash up front, he will give it to you if he thinks the risk is within reason. No matter what he might say, a dealer does have the financial authority to make this kind of deal.

I went to a car dealer on a Saturday in October. I wore faded blue jeans and a very elegant tweed jacket, to convey that "rich but casual" image. The one thing I did have was a fairly good credit profile—I live a lot of my life on credit cards. Even though I owe more money than several small countries, I always make sure to make the minimum monthly payments. So I'm always able to borrow money.

My salesman, Walt, was very helpful. I could tell he was the kind of guy who worked hard to see that a customer drove a new car home, even if it wasn't a high-profit deal.

As we picked out my car on the lot and I looked at the sticker price of $10,118, I said, "Hey! That's cheap!" to help give the impression I had lots of money to play with. Walt was friendly, and used some fun and harmless sales pitches. "That's a pretty car," he said, "a very pretty car." I had to agree; it *was* a pretty car, black and shiny with a great big sun roof. I loved the car, but I was resolved to buy it at a good price. I kept in mind my own rule about not being too eager to have your toys.

After I chose my car, I filled out the credit application. I didn't lie, but I was certainly confident and a bit creative. For my position, I put down something like "consultant", which I thought was fair, given all the people who ask me for advice about buying cars. (If I had put down "author," I'm not sure it would have worked. When people think "writer," they usually think "broke.") I put down my best guess as to how much money I might be making that year—I put down an optimistic figure.

The dealership ran up my credit profile on the computer. I saw Walt look over my credit report with his cold, sharp eye. I certainly had a lot of credit, and most of it looked pretty decent. But I could tell he was a little unsure of me.

I was very persistent in negotiating the price. In the

last chapter of this book, you'll find a step-by-step car negotiation that you can use as a model for your own triumph in the auto showroom. My own experience was very much along these lines.

The negotiation took about an hour. I acted simple and dumb, but friendly. As I recommend in this book, I just acted like I had some crazy idea about a big discount. Walt began by showing me the buyer's order with the full asking price of the car at $10,118. "If you'll just give your okay right there on that line, we'll finish up this paperwork and you can take your new car home."

"Walt," I said, "I think we can do this for a little less. I think you can sell me this car for about $9,200." I smiled and wasn't pushy. My freeze price for the small sports car I was buying was actually $9,504 ($10,118 − 12% ($1,214) = $8,904 + $600 = $9,504). I pitched the initial offer $300 below the freeze price so Walt could have the pleasure of bumping me up.

"I don't know if we can do that," said Walt. "There's just not that much of a profit margin in a small car like this. We can get you $200 off, maybe, but you're asking for practically a $1,000 discount."

I was satisfied that Walt had admitted so far that a discount was available, so I admitted that I might go up a little. "I know it's a small car, but my guess is we can do it pretty close to $9,200 if not right on the button. Here, I'll make the offer at $9,225," I said, and I wrote "9225" across the buyer's order and signed my name. I also put down my American Express card and gave it to Walt as a sign that I was a serious, good-faith bargainer, fully intending to buy the car.

Walt took my offer to the manager and returned in about ten minutes. "We've got a great price for you. The manager has approved the sale at $9,814—that's over three hundred dollars off. It's a great price."

"No," I responded, "I still think you can go a little lower. Tell you what, though," I continued, "I'll raise my own offer to $9,300."

"Look," Walt said, "We have to make a profit on this car . . ."

"I understand that, but I think $9,300 still has a good profit in it for you."

"We have to pay for the lights, the advertising, all the clerical staff, the kids washing up your new car right now. With just a few hundred dollars profit in the car, you can see how we've cut the price to the bone already." Walt was earnest, but I remained unmoved.

"You do like the car?" Walt asked. I nodded. "It's the right car for you, isn't it? Is there any reason that car isn't worth $9,814?" Walt proceeded to resell the car to me, hoping to build up enough appreciation in my mind to lead me to pay a higher price. After a long soliloquy on this topic, Walt concluded, "Really, $9,814 barely leaves any profit for us as it is."

"Okay, Walt," I said. "I'll raise my offer to $9,325." I wrote that figure on the buyer's order and signed.

Walt remained polite but shook his head. "You know I want to sell you this car just as much as you want to buy it."

"I understand that," I said. "But I want to get a good price just as much as I want to buy the car."

"Well, I'll take it to the manager." Walt went off for another powwow with the boss. After another long wait, he returned. "I don't know how you did it, but the manager's dropped the price to $9,637. It's incredible, and that's really a rock-bottom price."

"We're really close!" I said, a bit too excitedly. What the hell, I was thinking, what's 130-odd bucks? But I had my freeze price in the back of my mind—$9,504. And I am a man of principle. "We're really close. Tell you what, Walt. I'll go to $9,475 and I'm not getting bumped up any more. $9,475 and that's my final offer." Well, almost my final offer.

Once again, Walt talked to me about what a wonderful car I had selected. Once again, he told me about the dealer's need to make a reasonable profit. I stood firm: $9,475. I would go up to my freeze price, I decided, after they gave me one more discount. "Would you stay right here for a minute?" Walt asked. I nodded.

In a few minutes, Walt appeared with a large, amiable guy whom he introduced by saying, "Leslie, this is Mr.

——, our manager." The manager shook my hand firmly. As we sat down, I noticed the manager's almost magnetic charm and apparent sincerity. Once again I realized, these guys are good at what they do! "I understand," the manager began, "that we're only a little bit apart on making a deal here, and we'd really like to sell you that car. Now what can we do to get your business? We've got the right car for you, haven't we? And you know that we've got to make a profit too, don't you? We've given you a discount of nearly $500, and, let's see, your offer is $9,475, all you need is an extra $162 to drive this car home. That's about three dollars a month. You aren't going to let three dollars come between you and this car, are you?"

"Everything you say is true, it's the right car and all," I replied. "But $9,475 is my price and I'm holding firm." I looked the manager right in the eye.

The manager paused. "Well, all right, I can see you're a tough customer. If you say okay right now, I'll give you $100 off, let's see, that'll make it $9,437. How about it?" He offered his outstretched hand.

The manager had subtracted wrong! His previous offer was $9,637, and so $100 less is $9,537. I had already offered $9,475, and now he was offering me the car at $9,437! I began to laugh. Maybe it's because I'm so honest, but partly because I didn't want to win a price by trickery, I pointed out his mistake. "I think you subtracted wrong. Don't you mean $9,537?"

The manager turned red. "Oh—oh yeah, that's right," he said, both embarrassed at his mistake and astonished at my honesty. "Thanks very much. It *is* $9,537." I was still laughing.

"Look," I said, all smiles, "I just saved you $100. I think you owe me a commission on that, say 10 percent. So make it $9,527, so I've got the last word, and you've got a deal!" While I was still chuckling, we shook hands. The car was mine, and I was having such a good time embarrassing the sales manager that I didn't mind agreeing to 23 bucks over my freeze price. (The next time I bought a new car, though, just to prove the point, I hit my freeze price right on the button.) The manager left Walt to finish the paperwork.

It is very good to be a sharp negotiator. One of dealers' unspoken rules is that customers with bad credit *never* haggle about the price. If you're sharp enough to bargain down the price of a car, they figure, you're sharp enough to pay your bills.

"Walt," I said, "I'm making some important investments soon and I don't want to have a lot of capital tied up in a car. So I'll just put the sales tax and registration fees on my American Express Card, and let's finance the rest."

"We try to do everything we can for our customers," said Walt, who is really a very nice guy. The great thing about using American Express (MasterCard and Visa work, too) is that I would not have to pay that bill for another seven weeks: a month for the bill to arrive, and three more weeks to pay it. In those seven weeks, I was able to sell my old car to pay the credit card and make the first payments. Credit cards allow most people to make a "no money down" car deal. The dealer reports the credit card portion as "cash down payment" to the bank, but that's a fudge. It's hardly a cash down payment when you're borrowing money from the friendly people at Visa!

The finance manager said, "We'd like you to pick up the car Tuesday. We need to just check things out with the bank, get some financial references, you know, just paperwork. But the car is all yours, it's really all set."

"I don't know about that," I said. "I'll be happy to take this car home, *today*. But if we can't settle it right now, I think maybe I'll just keep shopping at some other dealers. Maybe I'll find a car I like better or a better deal. I really don't want to have to bother waiting for paperwork. I'm sure you can wrap it up now if you really want to, or else I don't think we have a deal." Now I was nervous. I was really aching to drive home that new car. It was now or never. I couldn't let them call for references because they might figure out I didn't have a regular job. They'd get cold feet. Once I took the car home, I knew they wouldn't want to chase after me to get it back. So if I didn't take the car home now, I'd have to start shopping all over again at another dealer.

The salesman, the sales manager, and the finance guy all went into a huddle. I paced outside like an expectant father. They bought it. They handed me the keys. "Congratulations, Dr. Sachs!" (I suppose my "Dr." title helped, too.) "Enjoy your new car!" I put over 1,000 miles on the new car before I paid a penny.

If you'd like to buy a new car with no money down, you are probably in a better position than I am. If you're like most people, you have a real job, which makes you an ideal customer in the eyes of a car dealer. Bargain aggressively on the price—that will impress them. Insist that they meet your terms, or you won't take the car. Chances are they'll give in, and if they won't, there's another dealer in town who will. Have fun!

10

Leasing a Car

"Hey, maybe I should lease a car," you might say. It sounds so sophisticated. Is it a good idea?

In the old days, only businesses and corporations did leasing. Nowadays, however, plenty of individuals lease their cars, and just about every dealer does leasing. All you have to do is ask. Often there is a special leasing manager whose job is to convince you to lease, and then to steal your money after you've agreed to do it.

It might be a good idea, but it also serves as a new and successful way of ripping people off. Here's why.

What Is a Lease Deal?

Leasing a car is basically a long-term rental. Instead of renting a car for a few days or a week, you agree to rent the car for three or four years. The dealer owns the car the whole time. At the end of your lease term, you may or may not have the option to buy the car at an appropriately reduced price. This option is usually not chosen: you don't want to buy a car you've been renting and beating up for three years, unless you've really fallen in love with it. Most likely, you'll go and lease another at that time.

When you buy a new car, you have to find some way to pay for the whole car, with your cash and trade-in and financing. When you lease a car, however, you don't have to pay for the car; you just have to pay for its depreciation. In other words, you have to pay for how much the car will decrease in value over the course of the lease. Plus, of course, the cost of tying up all that capital for four years, and a profit for the dealer.

In other words, if you buy a $10,000 car and make payments for four years, at the end of those four years you could have, let's say, a $4,000 car. But if you lease a car, you don't have to make payments on the full $10,000, but only on the $6,000 the car will drop in value, plus the use of capital and the profit. At the end of the lease period, the car dealer or manufacturer, not you, will own the car, just as they did at the beginning.

Advantages of Leasing

When you lease a car, you only "buy" the depreciation on the car, and not the car itself; therefore, your monthly payments are lower than the payment for buying the same car. Your lease payment might be roughly $20 a month per thousand dollars of car, versus $25 a month for every thousand dollars of car on a purchase. This can save you $50 a month or much more on your car payments, and hence the attractiveness of leasing. For cars costing over $20,000, the scale of savings is much bigger.

Since you are basically renting the car, you usually don't have to put up a big down payment. Leasing is often like renting an apartment: you put up one month's security deposit and the first month's rent. So you can begin driving the car of your dreams with less cash to start.

Since you are paying a lower monthly payment and little or no money down, you can afford to get a more expensive car. And that's the bottom line—isn't it?—to have a better set of wheels on the road. After all, your friends don't have to know that it's leased. After they see you in it three months in a row, they'll believe it's yours.

Leasing is perhaps the only way for many of us to afford big-ticket luxury cars. Note that you are paying for the *depreciation*, not for the car. Suppose a $30,000 car drops in value to $18,000 in four years; your lease payment only finances $12,000 (rather than $30,000!) and the interest on the remaining $18,000. The cost of leasing an expensive car that holds its value well does not rise as fast as the cost of the car. If you buy a car, however, your payment will go up in proportion to the car's value.

Disadvantages of Leasing

Although you can lease a car for little or no money down, with a lower monthly payment, your credit standing actually has to be *better* to lease a car. The reason is that dealers have to feel good about trusting you with the car without your having made a big investment in it by owning it and making a down payment on it. They will sell a car to almost everyone, but they're slightly stricter about leasing. (If you've got any kind of stable job, though, leasing is worth trying if you want it.)

It is harder to get out of a lease. In previous years it could be much harder, with the lease effectively locking you in to the car you had leased, particularly if you had a long lease term. In this case, your only option was to make a high enough offer to buy out the lease contract, which is not done as easily as making the payoff on a car loan. Leasing is not for people who expect to change their minds about the car soon. Nowadays, with more people leasing, and also wanting to lease a new car before the term on the old car is up, leasing contracts have more explicit, easier buy-out provisions.

When you lease a car, you are only allowed a certain amount of mileage per year, usually 15,000 to 18,000 miles. If you're going to drive more than that, you'll find that you are hit with a penalty for extra mileage at the end of the lease, a penalty that can run into many hundreds of dollars.

Leases, often result in arguments over the condition of the car at the end of the lease period. When you buy a car and finish the loan payments, it's yours, and no one can give you any guff. When you lease a car for four years, at the end of fourth year you have to pay additional charges if the car has exceeded the allowed mileage, and also if any unusual repairs are needed. You could be tied up in a large, unpleasant legal battle if you and the dealer disagree about the car's condition.

Finally, leasing deprives you of the psychological satisfaction of owning a car.

Despite lower monthly payments and little or no down payment, you usually lose money on a lease deal. The basic reason is that you get nothing for your money. When you buy a car, once you get out of the bucket, your payments build something for you: equity, the cash value of your car. It's an asset, which you can turn into cash if you want to. With leasing, though your payments are less, you get nothing in exchange for your payments. You borrowed a nice car, to be sure, but you pay money and you have nothing to show for it, not even a tax deduction on interest, other than the joy of using the car while it's in your possession.

Even though the leasing outfit owns the car, maintenance and repairs are still your responsibility in most leasing contracts. You're responsible for the car's condition when you turn it back in after four years.

At the end of four years, you realize that you have zero car to show for all the money you spent on the lease, and that you may have lost some dough over the long term. The basic reason to lease—the only good one, I think—is that when you're short of cash, it's the only way to get into the car of your dreams. When you get into the luxury-car category, the category of cars that cost more than $20,000 a year, it actually begins to make sense to lease.

Luxury-car leasing can make for a *big* difference in your monthly payment. When you lease a $12,000 car that will drop in value to $4,000, your lease will finance an $8,000 depreciation, plus an interest charge on the remaining $4,000. When you lease a $30,000 car that will drop in value to $18,000, your lease will finance only $12,000 in depreciation, plus an interest charge on the $18,000.

So you see, your monthly payment on a $30,000 car will be nearly 2 ½ times the payment on a $12,000 car if you buy it outright; but if you *lease* the $30,000 car, you only have to finance $4,000 more in depreciation than in the case of the $12,000 car, plus an interest charge on the $18,000 value that the car retains. But you pay none of the principal of the $18,000 residual value of the luxury car, and that is why the leasing of luxury cars can bring the monthly payment down from the outer limits of the galaxy into our solar system.

Leasing is a form of gambling in that the dealer who leases a car to you is assuming that the car will still be worth the said amount after the lease period is over. A lease can conceivably be profitable if the dealer turns out to be wrong: if the dealer assumes the car will be worth $3,000 after four years, and used car prices drop so much that the car is actually worth $500, you may have gotten a great deal. But it's unlikely that we real people will outfox a dealer at this kind of game. With the high profit built into most leasing contracts, I believe leasing should be avoided unless it's the *only* way to get into the car you want.

Why the Dealer Loves to Lease

Leasing has proven to be yet another wonderful profit scam for the auto-sales business. Salesmen love lease deals. I remember how overjoyed the salesmen would get when the customer said he wanted to lease; that way, a $1,000 commission was almost guaranteed! It was often sweet and clean, too, with no arguing from the customer.

There's no real reason why leasing has to be so profitable for the dealer, but like everything else, dealerships have it down to a system. It's complicated to figure out the financing when you're buying a car, and you know up front what the price is. But leasing is even more complicated because you're not financing a car but only the depreciation on a car. In order to do that, you need to know how much the car will depreciate and you need to guess at the value of the car four years from now, so you can calculate how much the car will depreciate in between. It's so complicated that dealers can often convince the customer that the lease price is fixed, that there's no argument, that this $237.90 per month bargain is just a take-it-or-leave-it figure. It's lower than a monthly purchase payment, so people often just swallow it.

As you might guess, the lease price is calculated from the *full markup* on a car. Sometimes dealers will even make up a figure out of the blue, just in the hope that you will sign automatically. After all, this talk of "depreciation allowance" and "residual value" (i.e., the worth of the car at the end of the lease period) is pretty mysterious. And they come up with their figures so cleanly, so crisply, so efficiently: the customer often assumes that it must be a fair price.

Even for the minority of customers who actually negotiate a lease price, management has found that they can "hold a much better gross" (profit margin) on lease contracts. Although a lease contract can be held down to just about the same profit level as a new car purchase, something prevents most customers from pursuing the matter too aggressively. Perhaps it's the fact that the payment is so much lower to begin with. Perhaps it's the fact that the calculations are so much more complicated. Perhaps it all seems so sophisticated that the customer just yields more to the dealer. But you can press a lease deal just as hard as you press a purchase deal. It just takes a little more work.

Deceptive Provisions in Lease Contracts

One of the things to notice about a lease deal is how very differently dealers handle the whole transaction. When you're buying a car, they push hard to sell you a $795 rustproofing. When you're leasing a car, and *they're* the ones who should be concerned about rust, they don't even mention it—thus by their silence exposing the rustproofing scheme for the puff of smoke that it is.

Leasing contracts have their own tricks, however:

1. You can make down payments on the lease, an up-front payment of cash (often called "capitalization reduction" or something similar) which will lower the monthly payments by a substantial amount. *Make sure that the payment you make up-front is duly recorded on the contract.*

2. The lease price is based not only on the car's assumed value and condition at the end of four years, but also on the expected mileage the car will be driven. Sometimes the penalty for driving the car more miles than expected is very high, or else the lease allows you so few miles per year you are almost guaranteed to pay a penalty. For example, suppose your four-year lease contract says the lease price is based on 10,000 miles per year, with a penalty of 10 cents per mile over that figure. That means that if you drive 15,000 miles per year, your penalty will be $2000 (20,000 × 10 cents). Both these figures—the annual mileage figure allowed by the loan and the penalty for going over that figure—are negotiable.

3. Some leasing contracts say that *you* have to pay the difference if the market value of the car is less than anticipated. A lease deal is worked out on the basis of a certain residual value of the car. The manager's calculations assume that in four years the car you lease will be worth so many dollars. The leasing contract will already say that you have to pay for high mileage, or unusual damage to the car, beyond ordinary wear and tear—that is bad enough. But the contract may also hold you liable in case the market for your kind of car is less than anticipated. What if 1987 turns out to be a bad year for you car, and four years from now its wholesale value is $1,200 less than anticipated? You don't want to have to pay that difference. Don't sign a contract like this—they're the experts, let them take the gamble.

4. I live in Virginia, where residents pay a personal property tax on their automobiles. When you have a new car in your possession, you can owe several hun-

dred dollars extra in tax for that year. You have to pay it whether your car is bought or leased. One of the very popular scams of car dealers is to raise the price of the lease on the grounds that it includes the payment of a personal property tax—when in fact it doesn't. Indeed, if you look at the fine print on the leasing contract, you will often see that the lessee (that's you) is responsible for the relevant taxes. So be careful!

5. Consider, too, the provisions, or lack of provisions, that make it especially hard or expensive for you to terminate the lease early if you want to trade in the car. Ending a lease is a bit complex, because the dealer or leasing company must now sell (or re-lease) this used vehicle long before the time they had originally expected. A lease is *not* a monthly rental, because the lease's profits are calculated over the full length of the lease. You might pay the same every month, but the leasing company makes more profit from the later months and years of the lease when the car is worth less. To end a lease early, you have to pay the leasing company for the profit lost through early termination of the lease. The lease contract might say nothing about ending a lease, which would leave you stuck for the full term or trapped into paying whatever termination fee the leasing company demanded. Alternatively, the stated termination fees could be so high they make it financially impossible for you to terminate early except by filing bankruptcy.

The dealer will offer you a lease contract; when in doubt, take it home and study it.

The Future of Leasing

As Americans get richer, used cars depreciate more rapidly. Americans seem to be prosperous enough these days to buy themselves a lot of new cars, and that means that the residual value of leased cars at the end of the lease term will be a lot less because of the lower demand for used cars. This means three things for you:

1. Don't sign a lease contract if the residual value of the car after the end of the lease term is not specified by the dealer.

2. As dealers and leasing companies become more aware of declining used car prices, the lower residual values will result in more expensive leases. (The value of the car goes down more quickly, and you have to pay for all the drop in value over the term of the lease.) If leases become just slightly more expensive, there will be very little difference in the monthly payment between leasing and buying of most cars under $20,000. Buying is such a better deal that you should almost always buy if you can afford to do it.

3. For a brief time there may be some real bargains in leasing, if leasing companies assume a high residual value for cars that are in fact going to drop steeply in value. Don't count on this, however, because the dealers and leasing companies will be very quick to pick up on this trend.

Leasing Companies

Nowadays, there are a number of companies in the leasing business. They will quote prices over the phone, which can be a big help in deciding what you can afford. Where do they get their cars from? From the car dealers in your area. Why should you use a leasing company? The only service it provides is that of finding the car you want at a specific dealer, with exactly the colors and options you request, and negotiating the price down to the level quoted.

If you're too busy to go car shopping, you don't mind getting a new car without test driving it, and you don't mind losing a little money, you will find that leasing companies can be a big help. Remember, though, they get their cars from dealers; which means that you can negotiate a better price from a dealer yourself because you don't have to pay the leasing company. It's mostly worthwhile to call the leasing companies for quotes so you'll know which prices are too *high*.

Leasing companies charge from 10 to 15 percent more than a dealer would to lease you the same car. On the other hand, people who lease from a car dealer often pay 20 percent more than the leasing company charges. Why this contradiction?

You can get a better lease price from a dealer, though a dealer who has you in his showroom will try to wheel and deal you into paying something absolutely outrageous. A car that a dealer will lease you for $200 a month for four years is one you can get from a leasing company for $220 a month. But if you go to the showroom yourself, they'll start by offering you a lease at $285 a month.

Leasing companies do much of their business over the phone, and give you low, competitive quotes because they assume you're shopping around. A dealer will gamble on convincing you to pay too much on the spot. The smart shopper will simply call two or three leasing companies, and then lease at a dealer for a little bit less.

How to Negotiate a Lease

It is really too big of a mess to calculate the perfect lease deal. You can find out what the dealer paid with my formula for determining the full invoice price (see above, p. 106) and you can add the appropriate minimum-profit margin for that car. But in order to calculate a lease price yourself, you must have accurate figures on the estimated residual value of the car (its wholesale value the month the lease expires), and the financing of the steadily declining depreciation over the four years the car will be held under the terms of the lease. That's a tall order.

The major difficulty in negotiating a lease is a psychological one. Salesmen and managers are accustomed to getting such incredible profit margins on lease deals that they have unusual expectations. Many of them have never made a minimum-profit lease deal, although they have sold a few cars to sharp customers at a low "gross." What I am saying is that, although they will negotiate a lease price, it is quite hard to budge them down to the bottom line on a lease. They just expect to make a ridiculous profit on every lease deal, and I have noticed a tendency on their part to refuse reasonable deals because of those expectations. This is true even when they would have sold you the same car for a minimum-profit deal.

So you've just got to hammer them, and do it at more than one dealer. Start by calling a leasing company, and then make sure you get a price that is at least 5 percent lower. If you feel you want to lease, and you want to do it at a good price, there is no substitute for just pounding on the dealer's head until he lowers the price. As you compare at various dealers, make sure that you are comparing the same car and same options, or as close to the same as possible; the same lease term, four years or whatever; and that none of the dealers has put something sneaky in the contract, especially if their price seems otherwise low.

Press for a lower price, and do your walk-away routine when they won't give in any further. After you've done the rounds, feel free to come back to the same dealer and beat on them some more. After it's clear you can go no further, and you're sure you can't afford to (or don't want to) buy the car, go ahead and lease it.

11

Some Extra Tips

There's really a lot of information to digest about the car business. The following are some information tips you might find helpful in your relations with the auto industry.

Dealer Service Departments

The service departments at new car dealers are dangerous places to do business. Many of them do have competent mechanics, to be sure. A dealer is especially likely to have someone who is very sharp at fixing problems on new cars, just in case a customer won't buy a car unless the problem that is discovered in the test drive is fixed immediately. There is usually plenty of talent on the premises.

But dealer service departments are famous for ripping you off. As with car sales, they usually have a service-with-a-smile motto, being as friendly as possible while they rob you blind.

The first rip-off of dealer service departments is their labor rate. Dealers' rates are often from one-third more to double that of an ordinary car mechanic. Many dealers charge $50 an hour or more for servicing a car, while regular mechanics charge $35. Why are they so rapacious? Because they have found they can get away with it.

Around 1980, when domestic car sales were slow, dealers worked hard to find other ways of making profits. They doubled the price of rustproofing, and doubled the labor costs in the service department. They found that it worked because they had a largely captive group of victims.

A lot of people think that somehow it is better to get your Pontiac fixed at a Pontiac dealer, your Honda at the Honda dealer, and so on. The theory is that the mechanic will be more familiar with your car and will have a better supply of parts. Many people will act on their gut feeling that the place that sold you the car is the best place to fix it.

Dealers also have a captive market because many customers are accustomed to visiting the dealer service department after they buy a new car. There may be some required checkups for the warranty, or "free" servicing that is offered at regular intervals for new car owners. Most of us are creatures of habit, and when we get comfortable dealing with one group of people (and they're so friendly, aren't they), we are reluctant to try someone new. So the customers keep coming back.

Sure, dealers realized, they would lose a few customers who realized they were being overcharged. But they more than make up the difference by earning double the charges from everyone else. It has worked out very well—many people don't even realize that dealers typically charge more for their labor.

Dealer service departments tend to rip people off by making work, too. Dealer management has found it profitable to give the service people bonuses for "discovering" new problems and "recommending" repairs on cars brought to the service departments. This is why even warranty servicing is so profitable for the dealership. Many customers have found that whenever they have brought the car to the dealer for some kind of "free" servicing, they always get a phone call: "Ma'am, we've taken care of that problem that you brought us. But we found something else wrong with your air-conditioning unit . . ." These other repairs are charged to the customer at the full price.

Another disadvantage of dealer service comes from the

sheer volume of their rip-offs. Many dealer service departments are entirely too busy to do the work you need quickly. Why would you want to have your car repaired by someone who is slow and charges too much?

My recommendation is to avoid dealer service departments like the plague. The rip-off mentality of car dealer management has its effect in the service area, even though it is service with a smile, "where customer satisfaction always counts." You can't expect the crooked sales managers at a dealership to leave the service area uncontaminated by their guile.

Only use the dealer when something is clearly covered by the warranty, in which case you have to be on your guard that the dealer doesn't "discover" some phony problem with your car that you must pay for out of your own pocket.

If you don't know a mechanic you can trust, I suggest you take your new car to one of the small service stores whose main business is selling tires. While there are still dishonest stores of this type, many are quite good and free of the car dealer's rip-off mentality. The tire companies check up on these stores, and they make their living by good service much more than a car dealership. Their labor costs tend to be reasonable, too, and the mechanics just as competent. Because the stores tend to be run by mechanics and not by auto-sales managers, they are often places where good mechanics like to work. Most of these stores are very good at handling all modern cars, though if you have an exotic foreign car you may have to shop around a bit. But *avoid* the dealer.

Auto-buying Services; Cars Direct from Europe.

Sometimes you will see advertisements of services that claim to negotiate a car deal for you at a rock-bottom price. They claim to have special relationships with dealers with whom they do a high-volume business, and from whom they claim to be able to win both the car of your choice and a good price.

You will find that these auto-buying services typically cost you more than you would spend if you negotiated for the car yourself in the style I recommend. After all, they've got to pay the dealer's profit as well as making something for themselves. Such services may also leave you waiting two months or more for the car you want, if it is not in showroom stock. Naturally, once you have put down a deposit and are simply waiting for a car to which you have committed yourself, you are a low priority to the anonymous dealer who has placed your special order.

The quickest and surest way to get a good deal is to win it yourself from the local scoundrels—it's the most fun as well.

Many import dealers in America can arrange for you to pick up a car in Europe. When arranged through an American dealership, the discount tends to be more modest (5 to 15 percent off the sticker) than if you just flew to Europe yourself and made your own selection and shipping and conversion arrangements. But the discount still pays for your plane fare; it's fun and convenient and the entire transaction is guaranteed by the American dealer.

If you're interested in a European car, you might consider buying it yourself in Europe. Given currency exchange rates and American dealer markups, a Mercedes bought in Europe can cost you much less, up to 40 percent less, than it costs in America. Even after you add a few thousand to pay for the shipping, and the conversion of the exhaust system to conform to America's strict antipollution emissions laws, you may have a great deal on your hands. There are a number of outfits, especially in the New York area and the West Coast, that specialize in conversion of European automobiles to American specifications. The discount will pay for more than your plane fare and European hotel bill.

A major problem with such "gray market," but legal, importing of European cars direct from Europe's factories is the number of conversion shops that do poor work, and wind up destroying your car while they fiddle with its emissions system. If you do go the do-it-yourself-direct-from-Europe route, find a conversion specialist who

(a) guarantees his work; (b) has been in business a long time; and (c) has good local references. If you are importing a car yourself, you take on the responsibility of making sure your car clears U.S. Customs, and this can involve delays of weeks or months: you pay duty on the car, and you will not be given final clearance to take possession of the car until the emissions conversion has been completed. It's not as easy as meeting the boat with your Mercedes on board, and then driving it away.

Also of interest are auto-buying services that advertise in the *Wall Street Journal* and the auto magazines, which will import a European car for you at a deep discount and take care of the conversion and Customs hassles. Some of these places are reputable, but some are not, and there is no easy way to tell with phone- and mail-order businesses. You will need cash up front, you will probably have to arrange your own financing, and you may have to wait awhile for your car. You also won't be able to drive your car before you pay for it, but you can indeed save some big money on expensive European cars.

Women and Auto Sales

More and more women are buying cars these days, thanks to their increasing wealth and independence. In some locales, the majority of cars are bought by women. It is taking some time, though, for women to catch up with men in their familiarity with car lore and the straight story on car dealers.

Regrettably, another increasing sign of feminine advancement is the increase in the numbers of car saleswomen. The sales managers I knew were desperate to hire women. Managers have discovered that unscrupulous women are very effective in the showroom. They can charm male customers as well as relax them: men are unwilling to believe that a woman could successfully take advantage of them. With female customers, saleswomen are successful in pulling the "fellow sister" routine, giving women a comfortable point of reference in a traditionally male enterprise. The few women I've met in car sales were working miracles in robbing the public. Some dealers even make a point of trumpeting in their advertising their female sales staff and their female management. But the crooked game is the same.

Purchasing a car helps establish or confirm many women's sense of independence. Car dealers exploit this ruthlessly and profitably. Women want their car-buying adventure to be pleasant, and are sometimes reluctant to provoke the hostility that is part of bargaining for a car. Women, more than men, tend to be unfamiliar with the car business, perhaps because of the tradition of car talk as a male activity. The sad fact is that women, who tend to earn less than men, also pay a lot more for the cars they buy. I hope this book has helped change that, once and for all.

Smart car dealers appreciate a woman customer, whether she walks in alone or makes a joint decision with the man in her life. I have seen salespeople approach their female customers with smoothness and pseudo-feminist respect, praising a woman's good judgment at choosing a car, conveniently omitting the fact that the next buyer might pay $2,000 less.

One traditional solution for women car buyers has been to take a man along. But this doesn't necessarily result in a better price. It's true that with a man present, the salesperson is less likely to resort to certain sales tactics. Men more often know that you can negotiate a car's price; thus a small discount will be forthcoming when the man insists upon it. But most men, like most women, are quite in the dark about exactly how much a new car price can be discounted. When I've seen couples in the auto showroom, the male has often been unwilling to admit his ignorance, and this male insecurity plays right into the hands of the salesperson. The salesperson will compliment the man on his sharp negotiating skill, and compliment the woman for bringing the man along, all to obscure the fact that the $400 discount they got should have been a $2,000 discount.

Car salespeople have a stereotype of the woman car

buyer as ignorant and gullible. They are often enough right to make enormously profitable lives for themselves. Their approach to women customers include the following.

The first order of business with any customer, besides convincing her to buy the car today, is to convince her that the price is set and that there is nothing to be negotiated. The major smoke screen used by salespeople is to compliment a woman's good judgment on picking out a particular car. This is very effective, as they are reaffirming a woman's independence and self-worth at the same time as they are preying upon her finances.

Saleswomen love to use the fellow-sister act, relaxing a woman who might otherwise be uncomfortable at a car dealer. Should the customer be knowledgeable enough to insist on a discount, the saleswoman will magnify the piddling discount she offers into a true sign of female solidarity.

Car salesmen also know the value of complimenting a woman's good judgment as a way of leading her astray. Bad car salesmen are clumsy enough to make crass remarks, but the good ones tend to know their market.

Car salesmen will, of course, compliment a woman's looks. Sometimes the salesmen will adopt a protective, fatherly air toward a woman, shepherding her around the dealership and through the lot. When they sense a woman customer's ignorance, they will use that fatherly approach during the price negotiation as a way to appeal to her instincts. Sometimes the salesmen will act hurt in order to induce feelings of guilt, and thus make her write a check. They will also resort to insults and intimidation whenever they feel these will pressure a woman into signing the sales order.

I've noticed that women car buyers have an excessive fondness for Japanese cars, even when the import of their choice is way out of their budget range. Many women, perhaps because they know less about the auto industry, have the impression that only Japanese cars are reliable, an important virtue to women more so than men. So some women who have modest incomes submit to the price gouging of Japanese-car dealers when more moderately priced American cars would fill their needs just as well.

Of course, women, like men, will enjoy the feeling of triumph that comes from getting a good deal. Women I've helped to buy a car have usually found a sense of increased independence as well as a healthier pocketbook.

I'm glad that more women are in the auto business. Women can appreciate the aesthetics of a car just as much as men, and are just as effective and professional in the business of auto sales and service. I only wish that auto saleswomen could be of a higher moral character than their male colleagues, but it would be wrong to put women on a pedestal, here as well as elsewhere.

When I was undercover in auto-sales school, there was one woman in the class. When we were out on the lot practicing sales pitches on each other, she was my partner. I interrupted our lesson and said, "You know, I'm really not sure about this business. I like the idea of selling cars, but I'm not sure I want to overcharge people by $3,000. I'm gonna feel guilty about taking their money."

She looked up at me and smiled a sweet smile, making me think that she understood, that she had a compassionate heart, that she appreciated what a dirty business it is. "Oh," she said, "I say take their money and to hell with the customers. Take all the money you can get!"

How to Get Revenge on a Car Dealer

You should, of course, make sure that everything is perfect about your car *before* you leave the dealer. The contract is not complete until the car is delivered to you, and so if you won't accept the car, you can count on the dealer to work furiously to see that things are done to your satisfaction.

The dealer is nervous until you accept delivery on a car, because he knows you can easily back out of the deal. Once I bought a car with a friend, and it only needed a set of louvers to be fully ready. (Louvers are those metal or plastic strips, usually black, that cover the rear window—they keep the car cool in the sun and add a sporty touch.) The salesman advised us to take the car home, and we would be able to get the louvers "in one or two weeks"—or, as I expected, after ten phone calls and a two-month wait. The salesman argued with us, the assistant manager argued with us, until finally they had a meeting in the general manager's office. I heard him scream: "Louvers, louvers, they want louvers. *So get them some* [obscenity] *louvers!*" The louvers arrived later that afternoon from the central parts depot.

After you get the car, drive it around for a while, and if there's something grossly wrong, take it right back. The courts have upheld a reasonable time period in which you can return the car for a full refund if the car is not what it is supposed to be. It's unclear what that reasonable period is, but a couple of days is a safe bet.

After that, if you've got problems with the car, be vocal and firm in your insistence that the warranty be upheld and that the problem be resolved immediately. Don't take baloney for an answer, and make sure that the problem is fixed before you accept the car back again. Recognize that you will be a low priority for the dealer service department. Even though dealers get reimbursed by the factory for any warranty work, the profit margin is not as high as on their own projects.

If your car has a problem that isn't resolved in two or three tries, it's time to consider two things. One is a lawsuit, which if filed promptly can be an effective form of pressure on the dealer. The other is to complain up and down the hierarchy in the auto business. The head office in Detroit, or the chief American headquarters of an imported car, are worth contacting. But the best people to yell at are in the zone manager's office, which is located somewhere in the area near your dealership. The zone manager deals with cases of gross customer dissatisfaction. When you write a letter, be sure to note at the bottom all the other people to whom you are sending copies. The zone manager also has the most clout in pressing your claim for recompense in case you've got a lemon—short of the courts.

The zone manager is also the person to contact in case

someone has been rude to you at a car dealer. The zone manager can kick your dealer's behind into the ozone. He is the one person who can punish the car dealer in the place that hurts him the most: his pocketbook. The zone manager can choke off the dealer's supply of cars, especially if there are some hot-selling models with high profit margins, fancy sports cars, or convertibles that the dealer would like to have. Complaints to the zone manager get results. If you let the dealer know you've contacted the zone manager, you can count on him to start sweating.

The zone manager, of course, doesn't give a hoot that the dealers are liars and crooks. Everybody in the auto business knows that, right to the very top. What they do care about, though, is that the cheating be done with a smile: they want the customers to be happy. They are a very effective source of revenge if a salesman has been rude to you. Make your letters to a zone manager brief and vivid—use phrases like "pompous little potatohead" —and send copies to the dealership's general manager. You can bet the salesman will regret having messed with you!

When you complain about a dealership, the zone manager will know that the dealer blew it, and he will take action to see that the dealer's fraudulence is more subtle in the future. Which, I suppose, is the best we can hope for in this crooked business.

12

Step-by-Step Negotiation Dialogue

You're about to buy a new Dodge. You saw a car on the street that you thought was cute and might just be your kind of car. You get in your old rustbucket and drive to the car dealer, probably "just looking," but checkbook in your pocket, just in case. As you pull into a customer parking space on the new car lot, you notice a few salespeople through the showroom window. They glance in your direction. One of them starts to head out the door and walk toward your car in an aggressive, forthright manner. You're ready, though, and you know that if you buy a car, you will get a good deal. The salesperson walking toward you appears to be slightly nervous, wondering if he will make a sale. But you're calm and relaxed, knowing that you're going to take your own sweet time and buy the car you want at the right price.

Step One: The Greeting

"Good morning!" says the person walking toward you with his hand outstretched. "Hi, I'm Joe Salesman! How can I help you today?"

YOU: Oh, I'm not really sure, maybe I'm just taking a look here.

JOE: Well, it's certainly a nice sunny day to be looking. Your name is?

YOU: I'm [name]. Thought I'd take a look at some of these Dodges.

JOE: (laughs) Well, glad to meet you, you've come to the right place. Is there one of the Dodge models in particular that you had in mind? (Joe will continue to draw you into light conversation as you look at cars. As long as you are looking for a car, and aren't trying to leave, Joe will be as friendly as possible while leading you around the showroom. Things will be very nice until you either decide to leave, in which case they may push hard to get you to stick around, or start to discuss the price or terms of the car you want to buy.)

Step Two: Qualifying the Customer

JOE: Do you live around here?

YOU: Oh, I live on Spring Hill, a couple of miles away. (Joe tries to guess your average income from your neighborhood.)

JOE: Do you have an apartment or a house up there?

YOU: I live in that Bonnie Gardens complex, off of Route 5.

JOE: Been in the area long?

YOU: Oh, about three years. The company transferred me here, and I told them I liked it so much I decided to stay. (Joe thinks: Good customer, stable job history, no question he can afford the car, no need to ask much more.)

JOE: What kind of car do you drive now?

YOU: I've got an '81 Buick Century, it's all paid up, I'll be trading it in. (Joe now knows something about what kind of car you like, how expensive a car you might be buying, how wealthy you may be, based on the length of time you've owned your car.)

Step Three: Getting Control of the Customer

JOE: So, you like the look of that Dodge 600, eh?

YOU: Well, sort of. I mean, it is a nice car. (Joe is getting you in the habit of answering questions with a yes.)

JOE: Just follow me. Most of our inventory of 600s is out in back. You'd like to look at a few, wouldn't you?

YOU: Oh, sure.

JOE: Then come this way. (Notice Joe doesn't say please; he just gives you directions, in a kind but firm way. You go along because you want to look at cars, but you know what game he's playing. Joe proceeds to lead you through various hallways and the service area.)

JOE: Oh, by the way, this is our service department. Anything your car needs, you'll find we have one of the best service departments in the area. Good service is important to you, isn't it? (You nod.) And that's why you'll be happy buying a car from us. (Joe is trying to get you used to the idea you're buying a car from him; he's getting you lost by leading you around the dealership to add to a feeling that he is the authority; and he is keeping up the flow of questions to which you answer yes. Finally, you arrive at the back lot.)

Step Four: The Customer "Lands" on a Car

JOE: Well, here are the 600s. There's a red one, and a black one next to it with a red interior. (Pause.) And across the way there is a two-tone silver and blue. And there's another maroon one. (Joe pauses again. The one time on the car lot when you will have a fair amount of freedom is when you are surveying cars in a specific category. Many customers will "land" on a car; a certain car will catch your fancy, and you will start to fall in love with the car that you will buy. It happens to all of us—even to car salesmen.)

YOU: What about that blue one? Is that a 600?

JOE: Indeed it is. (You both walk toward the blue one.) Yes, that's a pretty car. A very pretty car.

YOU: Hey, I like that padded roof.

JOE: Yes, the Dodge 600 Club Coupe comes with a fully padded roof, not just an ordinary vinyl cover. (He pushes the vinyl in with his finger to show the padding, thus starting to build the car's value in your mind.)

YOU: Yes, this is a very nice car indeed. (You walk around it, thinking that this car could be yours.)

JOE: Wait right there, let me get the keys, we'll take a closer look at it. (Joe memorizes the stock number on the window, goes back to the dealership building to get the keys.)

Step Five: The Presentation

JOE: Just let me show you a few things on the car. (Joe then begins a five-minute presentation on the features of the car in front of you. He circles the car, moving from one end to the other. The comfortable backseat, the roomy trunk, the attractive bumpers, the body-side moldings, the easy-to-reach dipstick under the hood, the fuel-injected engine, the maintenance-free battery. Joe often asks if you think a particular feature is good, as follows:)

JOE: Now the passenger doors have an extra steel bar in them for reinforced protection in case of a side collision. Safety is important to you, isn't it? (You nod.) Now just sit right down there on the passenger side, and I'll show you a few of the controls. (Joe leads you to the passenger seat, then turns the car on. This warms the engine up for good performance during the test drive that you will be taking. He turns on the air conditioning, the radio, and shows you the various gadgets on the car.) As you can see, the gauges are all easy to read, no matter what angle you tilt the steering wheel. Let's take it for a test drive, shall we? (Joe simply takes you on a test drive, without really asking you.)

YOU: Hmmm. Nice comfortable ride.

JOE: That's our special European suspension. Gives it an incredibly smooth ride. Behind the wheel, there's nothing like it. (You know Joe is being a salesman, but you do like the car anyway. Joe drives you a mile away, and then says:) OK, now you take the wheel, and enjoy!

YOU: Well, okay! (You get in the driver's position and adjust the seat to make yourself comfortable. You know that the radio and air conditioner work, and so you turn them both off to find out how smooth and quiet the engine really is. You start to drive the car.)

JOE: A thing you should notice about this 2.5 liter engine—"

YOU: Would you please just be quiet for a moment? I really need to feel how this car handles, and I just need a bit of quiet. (Joe shuts up, a bit surprised: your first bit of assertiveness. But you need to know if the car is right for you, not just if Joe thinks it's right for you.)

Step Six: The Close

JOE: So, are you enjoying this ride?

YOU: Oh, yes, quite a lot. This is a wonderful car.

JOE: I know it's a bit dusty on the front hood there, but we've got a great lot crew, they'll shine it all up so it'll really look like a new car for your friends. (Joe is once again getting you used to the idea that you're buying the car. You drive the car back to the dealer and pull it in the front. You get out of the car and stare at it. You're thinking about buying it. You know the moment of truth has come.)

JOE: So you like this car, huh?

YOU: Yes, I do.

JOE: So you like the way it handles, the way it rides, the way it looks, everything, right?

YOU: Oh, yeah, sure.

JOE: So let's wrap it up, and you can take it home, okay?" (A very long pause. Joe doesn't say a word, and he won't, until you say something. You stare and think, and finally you say it.)

YOU: If we can work out the price, I'll buy it.

JOE: Step this way, I'm sure we'll be able to work it out. (Before you leave your blue dream car, you make careful note of the factory sticker price on the window: $12,300. You note that the dealer has an add-on sticker, including: dealer markup, $995; rustproofing, $395; glaze and undercoating, $195; fabric protection, $135; bringing the total price on the second sticker to $14,020. But you know that the crucial number, for *your* calculations, is that factory sticker price of $12,300.)

Step Seven: Knowing Your Freeze Price

JOE: Just sit right down here, give me the keys to your Buick so we can have our used car manager get you a top appraisal on your old car, and we'll have a great price for you in just a few minutes. Can I get you some coffee or anything?

YOU: Yes, some coffee would be nice. (While Joe is away, you take out the little notepad in your pocket, and your calculator, and figure out the freeze price on the car you want. The factory sticker price is $12,300, and you use Dr. Sachs's magic formula: subtract 15 percent, and then add $600 to get your freeze price. $12,300 − 15% ($1,845) = $10,455 + 600 = $11,055. So you'll call it $11,050—they can certainly afford the five bucks.

But what about your old Buick? You've done a little research, taking your Buick around to used car dealers to see what they offer you. You found that because of the depressed used car market, the old Buick is only worth about $750. If you subtract that from the $11,050 you'll pay for the new car, you're left with a difference of $10,300 after trade-in. The amount of the cash down payment is random, and totally up to you—I recommend an amount that leaves a multiple of $500 to be financed, so that later, it's easy to check the finance math in a loan payment table. So you'll give them an extra $800 in a cash down payment, which means you'll have a new car loan of $9,500. From your research you know that banks are giving car loans now at about 11 to 12 percent.

So that's it. You'll buy this Dodge at a freeze price of $11,050. You'll get $750 for your trade-in, leaving a difference of $10,300. You'll refuse all the extras they'll try and sell you. You'll put $800 cash down, plus taxes, and get a $9,500 car loan at a rate no higher than 12 percent.)

Step Eight: The Negotiation

JOE: Well, it's your lucky day! have I got great news for you! (Joe takes a piece of paper out of his folder.) We can get you in that new Dodge, after we take in your trade-in, for a price of only $13,420 *difference*. Now just put your autograph right there, and we'll wrap it up for you! It's an incredible deal. (Of course, it's outrageous, but you're not too shocked because you've read this book.)

YOU: Actually, I don't think that's a good deal at all. My idea of a good price, with the trade-in included, is something like $9,900." (That's about $400 less than you'll actually pay. It's good to make your first offer about $400 below your freeze price. If you go much lower, they may think you're unrealistic and grow discouraged about you being a serious customer. At the same time, you want to give them the feeling of "bumping" you up in price a little, so they feel as if they have accomplished something.)

JOE: That's entirely impossible, much too low. Now, you do like that blue Dodge don't you? That is the right car for you, isn't it? You must realize that the price we offer is an incredibly good price for such a high-quality driving machine.

YOU: Oh, I have no doubts about the car. But much as I want to take the car home, I'm not taking it home unless I get the right price. And that price, including my trade-in, is $9,900.

JOE: Just how much do you think your trade-in is worth?

YOU: Tell me how much you're giving me for my trade-in.

JOE: Look, let me give it to you straight. I'm sure you like the car, but your '81 Buick just isn't worth that much. For one thing, the used car market has been pretty depressed recently—I mean really depressed. Your old Buick—there just isn't much demand for that sort of car. Plus it has a lot of problems. (Joe looks in his folder.) It needs new rear tires, repainting, transmission adjustment—the list goes on and on. That car isn't worth more than $300, tops. And our management is being generous with you in offering you double, yes I mean double, 100 percent more, a grand total of $600 for your used car.

YOU: Actually I've shopped the Buick around to a couple of dealers on this strip, and I know that car is worth $750. Without question.

JOE: Okay, okay, let me ask you this. If I can get you that $750 for the Buick, will you okay the deal? I mean, I'm not promising anything, but if I can get you your full asking price of $750 for the Buick, do we have a deal?

YOU: Well, actually, I think we have an even bigger problem on the price for the Dodge, and I think—

JOE: What's the problem? Is it monthly payments? Tell me what kind of monthly payment you're looking for, and we'll see if we can't work it out.

YOU: I want a monthly payment in the low or mid 200s, but—

JOE: Why didn't you say so? Hey, a payment in the 200s is no problem. Our finance people are great. A reasonable down payment, and some good financing, and we'll have you in the $200s, no problem. Just sign right here, and I'll add "monthly payment in $200s," and we'll have a deal, okay?

YOU: No, not so fast. Sure, even at that high price, with a big enough down payment, and a five-year car loan, sure, I imagine you can put it in the $200s. But I'll be losing a lot of money, both up front and down the road. Look, I'm only going to be making a small down payment, and we can't even discuss payments until we get the price right.

JOE: Well, the price of the car, as you can see, with all the options that I know you'll want, like rustproofing, fabric protection, glaze, and undercoating, is $14,020. And then we're offering you a great price on the trade-in, more than it's worth.

YOU: I'm buying a car, not all that other junk. No rustproofing, none of that baloney at all.

JOE: Why do you say it's baloney? Besides, the car has already been rustproofed, our cars come that way.

YOU: Whatever you say, I'm not paying for it, I'm just buying a car. (Joe proceeds for a while to try to tell you that rustproofing, etc., are real things that you should be paying for. He finally gives up.)

JOE: All right, what does it take to work out a deal on this car for you?

YOU: Counting the trade or not counting the trade?

JOE: However you want to do it. (You think of your freeze price on the new Dodge. The factory sticker was $12,300; your freeze price is $11,050.)

YOU: Well, I'm just going to insist on $750 for the trade-in, just flat out. For the Dodge, I'm willing to pay $10,800.

JOE: That's impossible, absolutely impossible. There just isn't that kind of profit margin built into the car.

YOU: Well, that's my offer. Here's my good faith. (You write out a check to the dealership for part of your down payment, or hand Joe a credit card.)

JOE: There's no way the manager is gonna approve a deal like this.

YOU: Well that's my offer. (You take the buyer's order, and write: "$10,800 for Dodge, with $750 trade-in for '81 Buick." You sign it.)

JOE: Okay, I'll take it to the manager. (Ten minutes pass. You go to the bathroom, and see Joe and two managers in a huddle in the manager's office. When you come back, they're still talking. You sit back down and munch on a candy bar. Joe walks back in.) Well, the manager feels that you're a very special customer, and we haven't sold that many cars today, so we're willing to make you a very special offer good for today only. We'll give you that new Dodge at the factory sticker price—that eliminates our markup, our profit, entirely—and give you $500 for your Buick, and I'm telling you that's more than it's worth. That puts you in your new car for only $11,800. That's absolutely incredible, and if I were you, I'd sign right now before the manager changes his mind.

YOU: No, that's still much too high.

JOE: Too high? Too high? Do you realize what a deal you're being offered? I can't believe you're passing this up!

YOU: I think we have to try this again. I know you're working hard on this, so I'll try and be reasonable and go up a little. I still want my $750 for the Buick. And I'll offer to pay $10,950 for the Dodge. (You remember that your freeze price is $11,050.) So that means I'll be paying $10,250. (You write that down on the buyer's order.)

JOE: I think you're moving in the right direction, but we're still a long way from having a deal. (He goes to the manager and comes back in a few minutes.) Well, I showed your offer to the manager. We're not even close really. He was mad at me, telling me you're not offering a good price because I didn't do a good enough job of showing you what a fine car it is, but I think you know what a good car that Dodge Club Coupe is. I just don't know why you're being so unreasonable on the price. But I've got a fantastic offer for you. You've made the manager do things I've never seen him do. He's offering you the Dodge for $12,000, that's $300 below sticker! Incredible! And he'll give you $700 for the Buick, leaving a difference of only $11,300. That's the best deal anyone's ever been offered at this dealership, and the manager just said to say, if we can't do it at that price, there's just nothing more we can do for you, so I better just shake your hand and show you on your way.

YOU: Well, I really appreciate the time you're spending on this, but my guess is, you can still budge a little more. Let me make *my* final offer. (You write on the buyer's order again.) I'll pay this much for the Dodge. (You write your freeze price: $11,050.) And I want the $750 for that Buick. That leaves, let's see, $10,300. And you've already got my $800 down payment. Have we got a deal?

JOE: No way. Can't be done. The manager's last offer was final.

YOU: Well, I guess it's good night, then, I'll just have to buy it from another dealer.

JOE: You mean, after all the time I spent with you, you're going to buy it somewhere else?

YOU: Well, I'm not going to pay $1,000 more than I have to.

JOE: We're only $1,000 apart, that's only about $25 a month or so on the payments. You going to let $25 come between you and a new car?

YOU: A thousand bucks is a thousand bucks. Thank you for your time, Joe. (You slowly collect your things, and begin to walk away, stopping to stare at a few of the cars on the showroom floor. Joe quickly steps into the manager's office, and then comes out to meet you, with hand outstretched.)

JOE: I don't know how you did it, but you did. You've got a deal.

Step Nine: Avoiding the Final Extras

JOE: Well, I'll make sure your new car is ready for you to take home. While they're doing that, just step right in here, and I'll introduce you to Suzy—oh, hi, Suzy—Suzy Extra, who will help you out with some of the care you'll be needing for your car.

SUZY: Hi, how are you today? I understand you just bought a new Dodge 600. That's a lovely car. I'm sure you'll be very happy with it. Do you plan to keep it a long time?

YOU: Oh, a few years, I dunno.

SUZY: Well, I'm sure you'll want to care for it, won't you?

YOU: Oh, sure.

SUZY: And you'll want to do everything you can to help your new Dodge keep its value, won't you?

YOU: Yes.

SUZY: Well, we have a special value for you in our complete Car Care Package . . . (Suzy delivers a twenty-minute sales talk trying to sell you various extra service plans and what have you, talking about the special prices available this week. You say no over and over again.)

YOU: No, and I mean it.

SUZY: Now tell me again why you don't want this plan? At such a great price, too.

YOU: Look, I've already decided, the answer is no. (You wait for a while after Suzy goes away. Then Joe comes by again.)

JOE: Well, did Suzy take good care of you? She always does. I think the finance manager is ready to see you. (Leads you to a back office, introduces you to a man sitting behind a computer.) This is Mr. Tom Finance, he'll clear up the final paperwork for you.

TOM: Oh, hi, how are you doing, that's a nice car you've bought. Here, sit down, we'll get this thing rolled up quickly. Okay, that's a new Dodge 600, trading in the Buick, let's see, price of $11,950 minus $750 for your trade . . .

YOU: You've made a mistake. The price on the Dodge is $11,050.

TOM: For a new Dodge 600? That can't be right.

YOU: No, definitely, it's $11,050. Either that's right or I'm leaving.

TOM: Hold on, just a moment. (Tom telephones the manager, pretends he's checking on the figures.) Oh, I guess you're right. Sorry about that. Five-year loan, right? (You nod. Tom punches the number into his computer and the financing sheet rolls out. Price of car: $11,050. Trade-in: $750. Difference: $10,300. Down payment: $800 plus taxes. But you notice that the amount left to finance, which should be $9,500 ($10,300 minus $800), is instead $11,350, financed at 15.5 percent, making your monthly payment $273.03. How come? You notice that the finance manager has re-added charges for rustproofing and the extended service plan, things you already turned down before, and that he has also added new charges for credit life and disability insurance.)

YOU: Hey, I don't want any of this stuff. (You take out a pen and cross out the bogus extras which you don't want.)

TOM: They told me you did. You mean you didn't want the extended service contract? I hope you realize what a good deal you're passing up . . . (Tom gives you the sales pitch again for these items, and also for credit life insurance, and so on.)

YOU: No, no, no, and that's final. Now, about that interest rate, that's much too high.

TOM: That's the market rate. Maybe we can discount it a little for you, but not much.

YOU: Banks are giving car loans at 11 to 12 percent now. That's a fact.

TOM: But they require large down payments, not the small down payment you're making here.

YOU: I put down $800, and gave a $750 car, to buy a car for $11,000. That's almost 15 percent. Besides, the money doesn't really cost you any more than it costs the bank. So I'm sure that you can make the loan at the high end of that range. Twelve percent, no higher.

TOM: But we can't do that.

YOU: Twelve percent. Or I buy the car somewhere else.

TOM: But it's a little late for that. You've already agreed to buy the car.

YOU: Not if you're going to charge me too much interest. I haven't taken the car home, and I know that it's not final until we agree on the terms here. Twelve percent, and I mean it. And make it a five-year loan. (Tom punches out the computer report, and the financing agreement comes out: $9,500 financed at 12 percent for five years, leaving you with a monthly payment of $211.34. Very nice, indeed.

If the finance manager insists on a higher finance rate, you tell him the deal's off. If he says, "Too late, you've bought the car," tell him you know he's wrong.

Demand that he consult the general manager. If you have to, walk away from the dealer and let them chase you.

But do be sure you're realistic about the interest rate. If necessary, use a phone at the dealer to call some banks, and ask them their rate for a car loan of the same length, e.g., five years. Don't pay the dealer more than one point over the average bank interest rate. He will not give up your car deal over that!)

TOM: Nice meeting you. Enjoy your car.

Step Ten: Driving Home in Triumph

JOE: Well, here it is! (Your new car is standing in front of the dealer, all shined up with motor running. Tom gives you a final rundown of the controls.)

YOU: Well, I know this wasn't a big profit deal for you, but I do appreciate your time.

JOE: The way I look at it is, a deal's a deal. I mean, a sale where you make $100 is better than no sale at all. One more sale is always extra bonus points, too. I'm sure you'll be happy with the car.

YOU: I'm sure I will, too. (And you drive into the distance, having earned the respect of Joe and the other people at the dealership in a way that few other customers do. And you've got a great car at a great price.)

Happy dealing!

Index